BILL JONES'
Further Notes from the
TURNING SHOP

BILL JONES'
Further Notes from the
TURNING SHOP

Guild of Master Craftsman Publications Ltd

This collection first appeared in *Woodturning* magazine,
issues 23–42, and was first published in this form in 1997
by Guild of Master Craftsman Publications Ltd,
166 High Street, Lewes,
East Sussex, BN7 1XU

ISBN 1 86108 036 0

The publishers would like to thank Tony Boase for his
photographs on pages vi,viii, 2, 9, 15, 22, 28, 35, 42, 49, 55, 62, 69,
75, 81, 85, 86, 94, 103, 109, 115, 121, 127, 133, 134, 136, 138 and 139.
Photographs of screwed box on page 52 by John Haywood.
All other photographs by Bill Jones.

Line drawings by Bill Jones

Designed by Teresa Dearlove

Typeface: Cheltenham and Simoncini Garamond

Colour separation by Global Colour (Malaysia)
Printed in Singapore under the supervision of MRM Graphics,
Winslow, Buckinghamshire, UK

Safety Note

The working methods contained in this book have been developed and perfected by Bill Jones, a highly skilled, professional turner, over many years. Descriptions of particular skills and general working practices are for historical interest – they are not instructional. Readers should be aware of safe working methods, and exercise common sense and caution in the workshop. Please refer to 'Health and Safety' on page 134 – your safety is your responsibility.

Contents

Left *Enlargement of pachyderm pendant.*

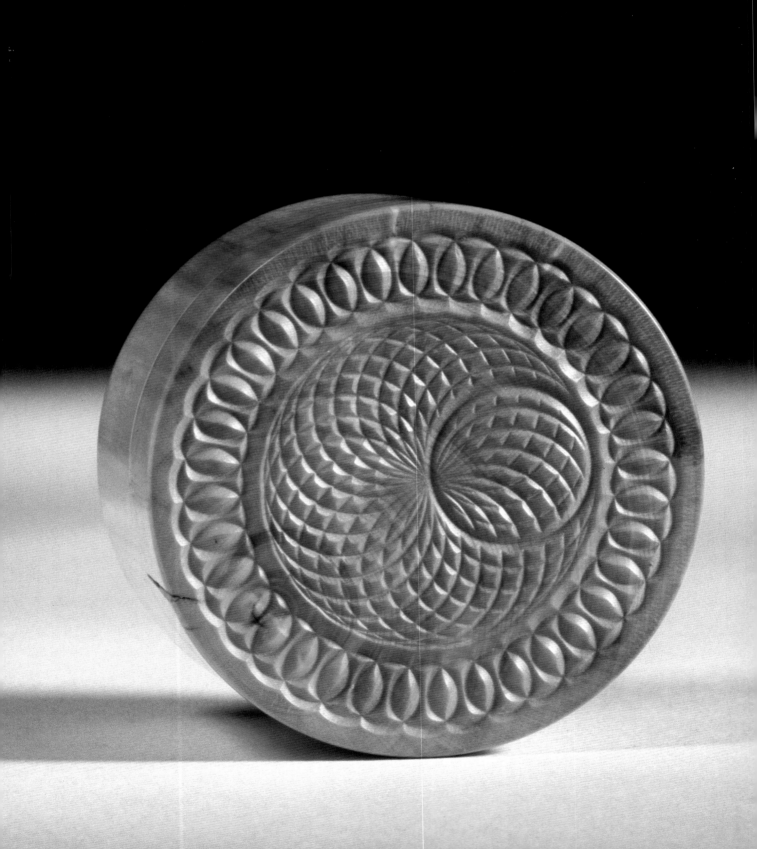

Introduction

I began my first book of 20 articles with a favourite piece of doggerel entitled 'Encouragement'. All my writing seems to have that word as its theme because I'm convinced that whatever skill one is aiming to achieve is attainable in a time commensurate with the effort one expends working at it.

If you appear to be making no progress after sincere endeavour, don't believe it; the good work will indubitably come, manured so to speak, by the sub-standard pieces that disappoint you. Without such low-grade work no-one ever made a masterpiece.

True, the occasional genius appears never to have had to take the trouble that most of us had, perforce, to endure whilst learning, but the truth is that what is easily attained affords us but little pleasure – to paraphrase old Dr Johnson. Indeed, I've known geniuses that were so bored with their effortless success that they didn't value it and pursued different work.

But the plodder who, tortoise-like, advances resolutely, will make progress which will bring delight. Further, the sure and certain accomplishment of hand and brain is, to those on our wavelength, a lasting pleasure that can never pall, but will go on increasing.

The impatient desire to make masterpieces can prove to be a stumbling block to progress because it is perseverance with simple work, until every tool movement becomes confident, that gives the ability to tackle complex things. Until that ability is evident, the finest work will prove elusive, if not impossible. But when the skill to turn a number of items exactly the same has become second nature, it will not only be fully absorbing and enjoyable, but your adventures into the realms of more ambitious work will be attended with far greater confidence.

Few want to practise as this implies drudgery with no end product except a skill that seems situated at such a distant spot on the far horizon that it makes you tired just thinking about starting. Well, forget the practice and start making things – simple things – trying to get each one a little nearer perfection than the last. I've been doing that for a lifetime and can assure you that far from becoming increasingly boring, as many would imagine, the reverse is the case. I am still learning, and have many more skills to master, the older I get.

Entre nous, I have a distinct advantage over most turners in the shape of a wife who scrutinizes my best work and finds faults I do not even know are there! I must thank her for this – annoying though it can be!

I hope you will enjoy a few more of my adventures in that most exciting of haunts – the turning shop.

Left *Barleycorn and Turk's head ECF patterns.*

Chapter 1
Starting OUT

Summer 1947. Friend Alfred, the landlord of my small workshop tucked away up a narrow passage in the Lower Clapton Road, used to drop in for his rent every Monday morning. Getting that shop in the first place is a yarn worth repeating.

After leaving the RAF the previous year, I'd been working at my old job in the shaving brush factory, but had been attracted by an offer to begin work after Christmas at a firm who wanted a chess set maker.

On Saturnalia's great day, 25 December, 1946, the postman delivered a present from my new firm. It was a letter stating unequivocally that, due to reasons that sounded fishy to me, they would not now be requiring my services. I was, therefore, 'up the creek', and I pondered with Olive, my wife, as I sipped my glass of Stones' ginger wine and puffed at my Manikin cigar, 'What the merry dickens do we do now?'

I could return to my old friend, Mr Brett, at

Boxwood catheter plugs.

the brush factory and doubtless he'd welcome me back, but dammit, I couldn't bring myself to return yet again, especially when I'd decided on something more interesting than brushes at a paltry fiver a week.

Forthwith I wrote to my father, Bertram, at the Cotswold village of Badsey, in the Vale of Evesham, explaining my position. He wrote straight back, inviting me to come up for a few weeks' work and to review the situation, a plan Olive and I embraced eagerly.

I enjoyed working with Bertram again, making the old familiar boxwood catheter plugs – 10 gross a week – while we discussed the future. We agreed there certainly should be work enough to keep me fully occupied if I could find a workshop.

I was keeping in touch with Olive from day to day and, after a fortnight, she'd spotted a newspaper ad. offering a small workshop. She went to enquire and found the rent was £2 per week, which we decided to accept, although it was double what it was worth at that time.

RENTING
I'm going to call the owner Alfred. He had a wealthy brother, George, who made a mint out of horn buttons and was well known to

Bertram years before. In fact, George had given me an ancient rifle when I was too young to lift it.

These brothers, George and Alfred, had a 95-year-old father still living, who was one of the real ivory turners and carvers of the last century, with a house in Clapton full of lathes, tackle and rubbish. He was an old colleague of my grandfather, Lewis Jones (1850–1914) and was his equal as a craftsman. Now, this ancient father of George and Alfred, the story goes, had killed a man around the turn of the century, by whanging him over the crumpet with a spanner. But, as the deceased was a double-dyed villain who preyed on ladies, the whole factory observed a conspiracy of silence, as it was agreed he'd done the community a valuable service. They said he'd fallen off the gas engine which, as a maintenance engineer, was quite likely.

Alfred, of course, was delighted to welcome me as a tenant, especially as he had an eye to the disposal of his father's gear when the old fellow snuffed it.

I don't mean to be irreverent, but I can see the old lad now as I saw him in '47, nipping up and down the stairs in his old house of lathes, shrivelled, but spry and agile and wearing a bowler hat, with a piping voice like that of Moore Marriott in the Will Hay films (you'll remember old Harbottle!).

MOVING SHOP

But I hadn't got back yet and was still working at Badsey. Bertram had quite a selection of gear surplus to his needs and he sorted out everything he could find – lathes, tools of every kind, motors, back carriages, belting etc., and materials too: ivory, horn, hardwoods,

Ivory cigarette holders.

plastics, odds and coconuts too numerous to mention. We made tidy bales so it could be transported safely by Pickfords carriers, and I hoped to get home as soon as may be for, at £2 a week rent, I couldn't afford to muck about.

However, in '47 we had a very severe winter – solid snow and ice until March, when a thaw set in and flooded much of the country. Day after day after day went by, and no sign of Pickfords. I was snowed up good and proper and continued working.

Of course, I was quite excited and keenly looking forward to running my own turning shop, but I was also anxious, having misgivings about my ability to do the wide variety of work that might be expected of me. I had seldom turned ivory at all and had no experience of cutting it – a bit like cutting diamonds, I felt. My only experience had been small turning and thread chasing.

Still, I had to begin, and the old man was behind me with help and encouragement. Whatever turned up, if anything, I could always pass the difficult jobs on to him, while he could send me work I could do. I hoped for the best anyhow and could hardly turn back – I had crossed the Rubicon.

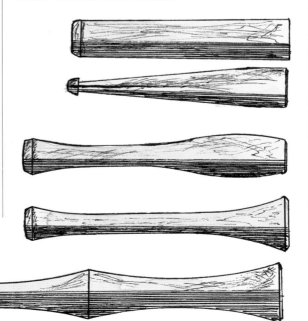

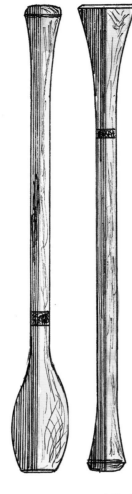

Two-piece ivory cigarette holders.

As the arctic conditions were clearly not going to shift, something had to give and, come February, Pickfords decided it was time they visited Badsey. As soon as the lorry came we loaded all the gear and I hopefully asked the driver if he could take me as a passenger. Although it was all 'agin K.R.s', he reckoned, in these extreme weather conditions, he could dig up a plausible reason in the unlikely event of some lunatic venturing out in snowshoes to enquire. I climbed aboard and, with the old folks' valedictory best wishes ringing in our ears, we set off for 'the Smoke'.

Through Broadway and up Fish Hill we went, huge snowdrifts several feet thick on either side of the road; they'd been there for weeks. We had a lively, but comfortable journey in spite of it and I alighted at the Nag's Head, Holloway, and was soon reunited with Olive.

Next day I called on Alfred, who welcomed me and showed me the workshop, a small, brick building with two floors, behind a row of shops in Lower Clapton Road. Mine was upstairs, a room about 16ft (1.5m) square with a central gas fire and a skylight, plenty of windows and excellent for my purpose, *but* – no electricity. I had to pay for a rising main to be connected.

SETTING UP

What with the usual snags and cussedness of getting anything done at all, plus the uncooperativeness of the people through whose premises the cable had to be taken, it was three weeks before I was ready to start. However, it gave me lots of time to construct benches from sound old timbers, 4 x 2in (100 x 50mm), and coach bolts at negligible cost. Also my young brother Bob – the one with brains – wired the shop.

Bertram too, came down for a day and treated me to more useful stuff, including a leg vice and shafting. I had a bench, 12ft (3.7m) long, with the vice at the right-hand end. My main lathe on it was a heavy, 8in (200mm) centre, which was used for turning, sawing, grinding, sanding, polishing, carving etc. The other headstock I had was a 5in (125mm) hollow mandrel with self-centring chucks.

Some lathes are good. One instinctively feels this and warms to them as friends almost at once. These two weren't good, but they served their purpose. The big one rattled and the other had faults that irritated. Still, the turner is a friend to all his tools and they become friends, warts and all.

The juice was connected when I was at the end of my patience. I'd been at the end of my cash for some time.

FINDING WORK

Alfred used to drop in for his rent on Monday mornings and stay jawing for a couple of hours. After a while, just as orders were becoming scarce, he put me in touch with a very fine firm of pipe makers, Adolph Frankau & Co., famous for 'BB' pipes.

They hadn't been able to obtain ivory cigarette tubes since before the war and were delighted to get my quotation. I worked out a fair price, added 20% to make it worth while, and got their order.

After the first delivery – and they paid pronto

– they allowed me to make all sizes between 2 and 6in (51 and 152mm) in ¼in (6mm) differences, just as my ivory would yield.

Usually, orders were for ½in (13mm) variations and definite sizes, so there was often a waste due to cutting down to a stated length. This made no sense, so it was a great piece of business to be allowed to make up whatever my ivory would yield.

SOME LATHES are good. One instinctively feels this and warms to them as friends almost at once.

Ivory has always been carefully conserved. It has been said that it doesn't so much get used up as that the pieces get smaller. From my old friend, Ernest Friedlein in the Minories, I bought hundredweights of cut points. The cut sections were 2½–3½in (63–90mm) lengths up to 1ft (30.5cm), all at ten bob a pound (450g).

The mouthpieces were shaped on the 2in (50mm) cutter by hand and finished in the vice with three flat files, coarse, medium and fine, smoothing with strips of glass cloth. The lip was finished on a sanding disc and they were polished on the buff to real pipe makers' standards.

Then on a bus, I met an old campaigner and comrade-in-arms from my RAF days, Arthur Bayliss. As an air-frame fitter (I was an engine fitter) he could handle tools and was happy to come in and do a daily stint filing mouthpieces for me. I suppose we continued for over a year pushing out these assorted tubes and making hay while the sun shone.

One fine day I took a parcel of them round on my bike – the firm was only a mile away. 'Ivory tubes from Jones', I announced, handing the parcel through the office window.

'Just a minute', someone said, 'We're up to here in ivory tubes.' It appeared they'd been stacking them away willy-nilly until finally someone had noticed. And that was the end of that, apart from the odd small order. I couldn't keep Arthur going either.

MR LOUIS

However, I still made tubes for a wonderful old character everyone in the ivory trade knew, he saw to that. Mr Louis started in the ivory piano key trade and was a jobbing ivory dealer and salesman of sundries.

In the early '20s, a huge ivory manufacturing firm, Bennetts, went bust. They had equipment, machinery, slabbing machines and the like, also ivory worth the proverbial king's ransom.

By some quirkish twist of fate, *all* the people who should have been at the auction sale of this valuable stuff were misinformed in some unfathomable way so, as luck would have it, only one astute little man happened to be there – our friend Mr Louis.

He didn't have a lot of money really, but it seems he didn't need it – there was no-one to top his bids, neither were there any reserve prices. Mr Louis bought a huge treasure of ivory and gear for a song and made a personal fortune that kept him happy and smiling all his life – and he must have lived to 90.

He could only totter and shuffle along and his wobbly hands had a violent shake. When he spoke, his voice was indescribable and difficult to understand until you got to know him well. He had a type of Parkinson's disease you see, but for all that he was a happy man with a nut brown head and the finest set of gleaming ivory teeth you ever saw.

He kept most of them all his life and swore by his dentist, Mr Harborrow of Harley Street. All the important ivory people went to Harborrow – a tiny man who crept up on his clients with his forceps hidden behind his back and stood on a box to extract teeth. 'If a dentist hurts you with his drill,' said he, 'take it from him forcibly and use it on him.'

By George! If Mr Harborrow were still with us we'd have more of our own choppers left, I promise you. And he was cheaper than the NHS. What isn't?

I'd known Mr Louis practically from birth (my birth), and he contacted me when he heard I was in business. He would spend many hours at ivory firms sorting waste ivory for suitable stuff to make ivory tubes, which I made up for him at eightpence an inch (25mm). Some were as short as ¾in (20mm) – I called them shilling shockers. He it was who brought me the first two-piece tubes to do.

They averaged 6in (150mm) long, trumpet or tulip, joined with a 4BA drilled brass screw, the pieces separated by a shagreen or black washer. They were delicate and beautiful, and it was vitally critical in the boring to avoid pushing the drill through the side or cracking the ivory when tapping.

Obviously, you would have the ivory of sufficient stoutness to take a 4BA tap without cracking, but Louis' ivory was often too thin to 'make' so, as his money was often the only thing 'twixt me and Carey Street, I made them 'make' – as many as I could. It became a fine art.

DON'T WORRY

In those days, before I'd become known, times could be worrisome as I didn't know where the next week's work was coming from or when I was going to be paid for the last job.

It was several years before I realized how unproductive and unnecessary worry was. I stopped it when I found that something always turned up and I don't believe there was ever a time when I hadn't a single job to do.

I tried to obtain work from various well-known firms and found a closed shop here and there so that, even when I showed a better sample at literally half the price they were paying, I didn't get an order – the 'old pals' society saw to that.

One old firm I approached, which had a reputation for making superlative hardwood, ivory, tortoiseshell and silver goods, asked me to make them a range of screw-top, ivory powder bowls from 2–3½in (50–90mm) diameter. What a test for a chap on the bottom rung.

I had a go and did them – not 100% perfect, but fine, saleable pieces I could show with pride. They pulled them to pieces unmercifully and, to cap it all, rejected them as too dear. I ask you, has anyone ever known BJ to be too dear? That was a costly example of man's inhumanity to man. Yet the days of these arrogant autocrats were numbered.

I was a young man in a moribund craft and the few highly skilled exponents that one by one retired or died,

Teething ring, rattle with whistle and screwed box – all ivory.

could not be replaced for love nor money.

Some years later that same firm lost its turner and there was no one else to go to but 'Jones the ivory'. 'I bet you told 'em where they could go, didn't you?', I hear you cry.

I didn't. I was as charitable as Joseph in Egypt. I ignored the past and they became one of my best customers for chess, backgammon, draughtsmen, condiment sets, peppermills, shoelifts, manicure boxes, chairmans' hammers, gavels, rattles, teething rings, spoons, repairs, ad infinitum.

ACQUIRING TOOLS AND EQUIPMENT

Then along came McDermott, who was running a new business with a dozen small capstan lathes, making ball point pens in erinoid – a casein material kinder to turners and superior to most of today's plastics. He wanted me to hand-finish the ends of the drilled and screwed pens – thousands of 'em. They were easiest to do using a Jacobs chuck, which only needed tightening by hand, so I got an engineer to fit one on the hollow mandrel.

Erinoid pen end.

After a fortnight McDermott told me, 'It would pay you to buy a new Acorn Capstan headstock.' The one he advised had a 3½in (90mm) centre, with Timkin taper roller bearings and a quick-closing collet mechanism.

This meant that the collets could be operated without stopping the lathe. I bought a new one for £25 – quite a lot in those days – raised it to 5in (125mm) centre on beech blocks, and had two chucks fitted; a 4in (100mm) three-jaw, self-centring, geared scroll, and a 3in (75mm) three-jaw, lever scroll. It had a ⅝in (15mm) hollow mandrel, was

rock steady and has been the most useful piece of lathery I've ever bought. It paid for itself with the pen work alone in a few weeks.

It's been running almost daily for over 40 years without the slightest fuss or defect, and was a tremendous improvement on my other lathes for accurately drilling tubes.

Alfred was always bringing me bits and pieces of junk from his father's house and asking rather more for them than they were worth. When the old man died his grandson, before anyone knew, got a local scrap merchant to clear the house.

Alfred dashed up my stairs in great excitement . . . 'Mr Jones!' he cried, 'Rush round to the Southgate Road scrapyard. My son's had all the tools carted there, but I've rung the proprietor and he will let you sort out whatever you want.'

I rode round on my bike and sorted out a bagful of handy tools and turner's bits and bobs you probably wouldn't pick up in the street, and Alfred charged me for each and every one. I never met a skinflint to beat him. He was almost tearful but, in truth, his son had done the wise thing, as that house might never otherwise have been cleared.

MOVING AGAIN

Soon after this I had an opportunity to move back to De Beauvoir town – two doors from the house my family occupied until the war. I obtained a workshop there at half the rent I was paying Alfred, and in far pleasanter surroundings. It was to be one of the happiest decades of my life. The shop was 8 x 20ft (26 x 65.5m), with a spacious back garden.

A letter from the redoubtable Bertram dated 12 July, '49 read: 'Glad to hear you're going on all right with your new shop. Have some cards printed and send to all customers saying, "Owing to tremendous demand for ivory goods we are removing to more spacious premises" etc. '

Chapter 2
Befriending Your TOOLS

I was reading something a colleague had written a while back, to the effect that when demonstrating on one occasion, he was relieved to find the lathe didn't 'play up', as other turners were watching and it would've been infra dig to be caught fumbling for tommy bars, spanners, etc., in an effort to discover how the dickens the tool rest locked and unlocked.

It reminded me of an ancient Frank Richards story about 'Squiff', alias Samson Quincy Iffley Field, the New South Wales junior of the Remove at Greyfriars School.

When travelling to the school on his first term (around 1910), he was observed reading a book entitled *Cricket for Beginners*, he was assumed to be 'green' at the game. It was a while before he was prepared even to play,

Above *Boxwood sphere, and assorted favourite tools.*

and he was presumed to be a dud. However, he got himself into an important match with the largest audience, the whole school, waiting to roar their heads off with laughter . . .

He ambled to the wicket – the usual '10 to make and the last man in' situation – apparently uncertain which end of the bat to grasp. He prepared to receive his first ball by stooping over the bat in a stiff, bent posture as though deformed. The school rocked with laughter and a few catcalls were heard.

The bowler wasn't fooling – he sent down a sizzler which whizzed past Squiff, causing him to shy like a startled horse, brandishing his bat ineffectually in the air. The next ball was right on target, but, as it left the bowler's hand a transformation occurred.

Straightening up in an instant, Squiff assumed the stance of a born batsman and slogged it – for six of course! Thus, Squiff made his never-to-be-forgotten debut, proving that it doesn't do to make hasty judgements. Mozart admitted to doing a 'Squiff' before playing the fiddle – which he really could play.

IDIOSYNCRACIES

Lathes are a bit more complicated than bats, and there's not the slightest blame to be attached to one who happens to be unfamiliar with their inscrutable workings. Some seem to have been purposely designed to intimidate the uninitiated, or to encourage the initiated to think he's doing something clever. Being an ancient old buffer – in years only – it don't work with me because I reckon that age is entitled to a few mild eccentricities.

I never shift the tool rest on a strange machine without moving the lever in the wrong direction first – sometimes deliberately. Some levers work equally badly in either direction.

Likewise, the shifting of the driving belt up or down, to change speed, is fraught with chance, and I often get it wrong until I get used

to it, which may take the best part of the day.

This is because I'm slow on the uptake: not a disadvantage according to Walter Savage Landor (1775–1864) who said, 'Quickness is among the least of the mind's properties . . . the liar has it, the cheat has it; we find it on the racecourse and at the card table; education does not give it and reflection takes away from it.' Isn't that encouraging?

DEMONSTRATIONS

Nobody knows whether I'm quite serious or not when I start adjusting a 'demo' lathe – least of all *me* – but the audience seem to like it and they rise to the occasion.

I have hoards of helpers who dash out from all directions to put me right, I'm glad to say. I usually find at least one good friend who stands at the ready to pick up all the tools that fall off the lathe bed with sickening regularity, bashing the point of a screever or point tool on the concrete deck.

One of these 'fielders' was most helpful, by unearthing a sheet of hardboard and laying it underneath to catch the tools on one occasion. I'm sure the audience is vastly encouraged to find that the demonstrator is human too. Some turners, watching for a miracle-worker, and half inclined to chuck the whole business in disgust, perk up unmistakably as they see me fooling about, finding difficulty in doing the simple things they can do on their heads.

SOME turners perk up unmistakably as they see me fooling about, finding difficulty in doing the simple things they can do on their heads

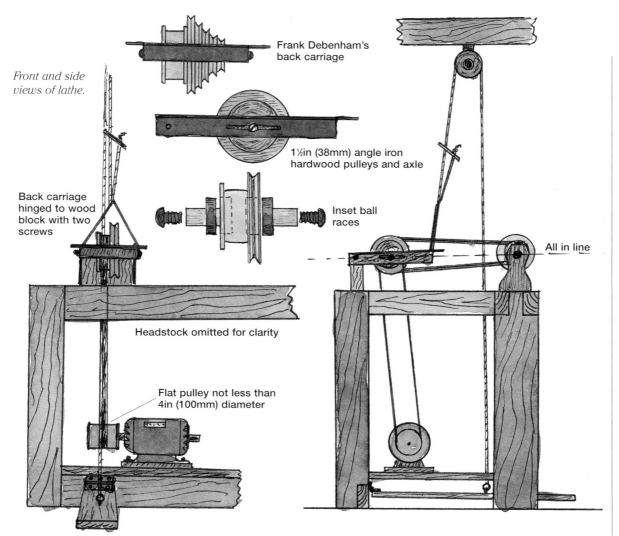

Front and side views of lathe.

Frank Debenham's back carriage

1½in (38mm) angle iron hardwood pulleys and axle

Back carriage hinged to wood block with two screws

Inset ball races

All in line

Headstock omitted for clarity

Flat pulley not less than 4in (100mm) diameter

And if they laugh I only laugh louder – at myself, but also at these modern times when they've scrapped many of the ideas that made sense. They haven't even a place to put tools without them falling off. The fact that I usually press the wrong button three times out of five is not lost on my audience and ensures their empathy.

VARIABLE-SPEED LATHES

On many modern machines, you can't change speed or stop the lathe while actually turning. You usually have to stop to vary the speed on a variable-speed lathe, and even that facility is frightfully costly. Mine works by foot pedal and costs comparatively nothing.

A brilliant ornamental turner I know was up among the Birmingham turners recently and described my back carriage and slipping belt variable-speed arrangement to them. They were scathing in their disbelief. 'It wouldn't work,' they averred, 'not on *real* lathes.' To them, I imagine, the pole lathe is a myth.

Strangely, Bertram told me, the idea actually originated in Birmingham. We always used it, but I've no idea if anyone else is using it now. I have given details of its simple construction a number of times, but to my knowledge not one person has attempted to make it.

I would have expected a few members of the Society of Ornamental Turners to have a shot, because a fair number enjoy making the most complex machinery, some requiring the highest ability in precision engineering. In

11

fact, many enjoy making tools far more than actually using them.

Around 1958, one member of the Society, Professor Frank Debenham (a geologist on Scott's famous Antarctic expedition) did adopt my method of variable speed for his Evans ornamental lathe.

I made the back carriage for him and fitted it with mahogany stepped pulleys to match his lathe. I do not use stepped pulleys on the back carriage myself, but certainly it would be advantageous if low speeds were wanted at full power.

Professor Debenham died a little later, in his eighties, but I have an old letter from him which says:

'I am fairly busy sitting at my desk all day trying to control a very pleasant team of four girls and two men engaged on designing a new atlas.

'It is fun, but I confess that I would rather be standing at my lathe, turning ivory, with the help of the loose belt contrivance which I learnt from Bill Jones.' A great Aussie.

Many modern lathes are closed in for some inscrutable reason, which can be remedied by judicious work with a hacksaw. But, seriously, there are plenty of open plan lathes knocking around, to say nothing of the excellent Conover lathe which is a beauty.

Does the apparatus work? Having used it all my working life, isn't that question absurd? You have only to look at it to see how practical it is. If it doesn't function well, there are several points of adjustment that should set it going sweetly and ensure efficiency.

Is it 'man enough for the job?', as the Cornish say. It is as strong as its components and motor, so it's up to you. Not being a heavyweight specialist, my tackle is fairly light, yet for heavier jobs I can still nurse it along by taking lighter cuts.

In any case, I've seen turners forcing their tools with all their power, impatiently, to grind the wood to shape, half stopping the lathe, as if the man who made time hadn't made enough for him.

I don't call that cutting wood as it prefers to be cut, or even as it doesn't mind being cut, to use Frank Pain's expressions. How lovely to watch a turner cutting wood cleanly, evenly and incomparably skilfully. He don't stop the lathe with the force he uses, and if he takes a bit longer – which isn't always the case – the whole operation is a joy to all concerned, machinery and wood.

And what about the *real* lathes they referred to? Some have electronic variable speed – which I found very good. When you find you can slow the lathe, or stop it with a heavy cut, you have to stop turning while you twiddle a knob.

But there are no knobs and switches on my variable-speed lathe. As you feel the tool slowing the lathe, your foot depresses the pedal by reflex action – easy as accelerating in a car – and the extra power is there without even having to think about it.

BELTS AND DRESSINGS

You would think the 1in (25mm) flat leather belt would quickly wear out, but strangely, it doesn't. It lasts half a lifetime. I keep a block of black belt dressing which I apply to the moving belt when I need extra grip, such as on cold mornings, before my taper roller-bearings have thawed. The block of dressing lasts as long.

The arrangement for belts is as follows. When the hinged foot pedal is hard down there is a straight line through the back carriage hinge, the back carriage pulley axle and the lathe mandrel. This is adjusted by the length of the flat belt. The lathe driving belt is adjusted by tightening the axle at the best position in the slots cut in the angle iron.

At top speed, when the belts are both taut, the front angle iron of the back carriage is exactly midway between the lathe driving belt.

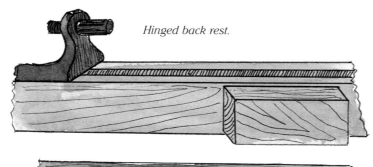

Hinged back rest.

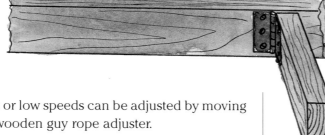

High or low speeds can be adjusted by moving the wooden guy rope adjuster.

This is essentially a non-precision lash-up, like the kids' scooters we used to make with timber and large ball races for wheels – some of them were quite sophisticated, commensurate with the ingenuity of the maker.

Any ropes, pulleys, brackets, wood and iron that you find may make your variable-speed different but, if soundly constructed, they most certainly work. Like messing about in boats, messing about with the time-honoured variable-speed slipping belt is a most pleasurable pursuit which won't fail. This one contrivance can make a poor turner good, a good turner better and a screw cutter happy.

There's no doubt the old turners had the best of it. They knocked up their sturdy timber benches, with tons of room for all their tools and work behind the lathe, where it wouldn't fall off.

They also had a hinged back rest, situated about 2ft (600mm) to the right of the headstock, to lean back on when boring or hollowing etc., so straddling the lathe would be quite unnecessary.

HOME-MADE TOOLS

Tuesday, 19 November, '91 . . . I have some sample napkin rings to make from a length of alternative ivory (polyester resin) supplied. Back in the twenties, Bertram, browsing around the metal stockists and other emporia of Clerkenwell, found the yard of a firm that sold weldless steel tubing.

I don't know if they thought Bertram was likely to place a shipping order for some – he may possibly have given that impression – but he got the yard man to oblige him by cutting nine 6in (150mm) lengths from $^{11}\!/_{16}$–$1^{15}\!/_{32}$in (17–47mm) diameter, for trepanning ivory.

I still have them, and the smaller sizes have been well used. They aren't very easy to push through ivory. The steel is about $^{3}\!/_{64}$in (1mm) thick, and saw teeth are filed, six or seven to the inch, fairly coarsely, and set for clearance. A wooden handle is fitted to the other end, and before beginning the cut, a recess to fit the saw is made with a screever (small parting tool). You feed the saw in entirely by feel.

It's hard work, and you have to clear it constantly. Sometimes it goes well, at others you just have to persevere until you win. Force mustn't be used or it can seize up. You mustn't allow it to get too hot or the ivory can crack – audibly.

I was coring an ivory peppermill with a tubular saw of ¾in (19mm) diameter a while back, when it crumpled in the middle and came apart. It had been in regular use for half a century and had rusted through because it

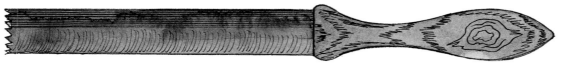

Tubular saw.

had been water lubricated most of the time.

Well, to hollow out solid ivory was unthinkable. I put the word round and by and by three tubes were delivered, all too thick, and no-one available to turn one down for me.

But by then it didn't matter because I had remembered seeing an old cycle handlebar, with straight ends, in a local hedge. The inside diameter was right – ¾in (19mm) – so I cut my length, then turned, filed, scraped and hacked it down to size, set it, and since then have used no other.

The steel was terrible, hence the difficulty, but I reckon it will last for years. I used them a lot for organ stop bushes and peppermills, but never napkin rings, because hollow scrivelloes were always used, not solid.

This time it was alternative ivory. I found a 1⅛in (30mm) tube and quickly turned a fine handle out of my stock of willow. The saw

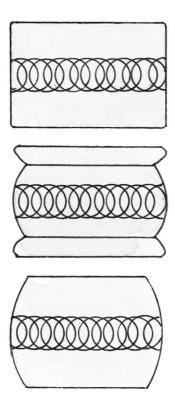

Alternative ivory napkin rings.

hadn't been touched for decades, but it went through alternative ivory like cheese.

I took it halfway, reversed it, and met it from the other end, finishing with a length of 1in (25mm) rod, which I tapped out of the saw. I made my three samples and polished them.

I wanted to make a simple decoration around the middle of each, with the eccentric cutting frame tooled with a 60° point tool at ¼in (6mm) radius. I have a screw-on, boxwood, tapered mandrel, and a rub of chalk ensures that rings can be tapped on truly with my magic boxwood hammer, and they should hold on . . .

If one does, for any reason, shift under the onslaught of the eccentric cutter, it will not only be chipped or spoilt in some way, but 'twill be next to impossible to replace it in the precise position again.

Sure enough, the middle one did shift, and a trifling dig was inflicted. I tapped it straight back – of course I did – fitted the point tool as close as possible into the last ring I'd cut.

That, fortunately, matched one of the holes in the row I was using on the division plate. The pattern of 24 circles was completed. The slight defect will illustrate to the prospective client that there is risk attached to ornamental turning, so it is not money for old rope.

Supposing you wished to chuck them more safely for the decoration. One way would be to cut a screw in the hole. Then, each ring could be turned and decorated on a screw adapter and the finishing of the inside done afterwards.

In fact, I think that's what I'll do because, although alternative ivory is easier to use than the real thing, in some ways, ivory wouldn't have come unshipped, because it's tough enough to have been clouted on harder.

Before leaving the subject, I should mention that in the case of using the tubular saw on ivory, a more positive grip is essential. To this end, a hole is drilled through the meaty end of the handle for the use of a tommy bar.

Chapter 3
A *Turner's* WORK

*I*n the last instalment, I rashly praised the longevity of my flat leather belts: a couple of weeks later my main one broke. It had worn quite thin and the chamfered join had parted.

Fortunately, I had some new 1in (25mm) belting and I set about cutting it to the correct length, taking the measurement of the old, so that when taut, the front bar of the back carriage would be no higher than the middle of the lathe driving belt. Should it be so, the driving belt gets too tight.

The new belt didn't go right for a while, because it was stiff and needed a bit of running in. Also, it stretches, so I had to shorten it a little on two occasions. But within a day it settled down. I thought I'd mention this episode in case someone tries making the BJ variable-speed machine and finds it reluctant to function at first.

I also needed my block of belt dressing, which makes the belt grip until belt and pulleys are getting on beautifully together. One rare advantage with my variable speed is that you can put faults right at no cost.

BELT FASTENING METHODS

There are several different belt fastening methods. The one shown below has to be hammered home, one each end of the belt, and is joined by a special pin. The pin has to be in position when driving the lugs home, and I find an initial squeeze in the vice to start it helps.

Leather belt fastened by hammering each end and securing with special pins.

Speaking of belts and belting, that good friend and fine turner, Roger Davies, has provided the name of a firm of power transmission engineers who can supply pulleys, gear wheels bearings, belts flat and round, etc. It is: Mountains Ltd, Unit 7, Haysbridge Business Centre, Brickhouse Lane, South Godstone, Surrey RH9 8JW.

One way to fasten flat belts is by cutting vees in the leather, as illustrated above right, and tying firmly with good twine. Mason's line is fine for this and I'm never without it. It is useful for running cutting frames from the overhead.

Normally I use spliced ⅛in (3mm) rope, but when belts of a different length are required in certain circumstances, a bit of mason's line, tied as shown right, can solve the difficulty very well.

The poor man's belt fastener – string.

LOOSE TEETH

I have also, on three occasions, found it efficacious in the painless removal of very loose teeth. It works perfectly in the following circumstances: 1 the tooth must be loose; 2 it must be bigger at the crown so that a slip knot will not pull straight off; and 3 you must be fit and venturesome enough to do the unconventional thing occasionally.

I have a loft with a large opening. I stand up there with the floor 11ft (3.4m) below. I have a 5lb. (2.3kg) weight suspended on 8ft (2.4m) of mason's line. The other end is tied firmly to the tooth with a slip knot.

There is something to break the fall of the weight as it hits the floor, such as a cushion from an armchair. The weight is placed by the right foot on the edge of the loft opening, the line free from tangles.

Double reef knot.

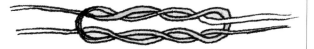

I hold on to an overhead timber, firmly, a piece of clean cotton wool in my right hand. Then, without thinking about it or shilly-shallying, my right foot pushes the weight off on its swift journey to the deck below.

I feel a jolt as the line tightens, stretches and instantly whips out the tooth. Then I place the cotton wool in the cavity and bite on it. That's all! My wife has a couple of loose teeth, but can I persuade her? Of course, I wait until I am alone in the house, in case I brain someone.

LOVE OF TURNING

Writing for *Woodturning* has transformed my life, and at a time when most men have long been retired. Many earn a living at turning, without it becoming more than a living. But for those who enjoy the atmosphere of the turner's workshop, there can be no retirement while health and opportunity last.

Bertram (1885–1969).

Old Bertram (though he never grew old) died at 84, but might have lasted longer had not a 'friend', who admired his facility with beautiful turned and carved trinkets, always hinted he'd like to have the little Leicester headstock. This was the sole remaining lathe used by Bertram in his final workshop – an ex-pantry, 5 x 5ft (1.5 x 1.5mm).

In an unguarded moment, when he was a bit low and rheumaticky, he parted with the lathe. The man thought it was the lathe that did the work.

Come the spring, when orders arrived for small gifts or repairs that would have been a pleasure and therapy to do, Bertram realized he'd been a bit hasty.

He didn't linger long after that, and I'm sure he'd have had a year or two longer had his old friend still been rattling round to keep him occupied.

Twenty years later, I saw the old blacksmith, Mr Caswell, at his forge 200 paces from Bertram's workshop. He knew me at once, altho' he hadn't seen me for 40 years. 'It's like looking at Bertram,' he said. 'If I was talking to him in his shop while he was turning, he'd look up at me and still keep on turning. He was a marvellous craftsman.'

He was glad to hear I was following the family tradition. The smith, at turned 80, was also keeping his hand in, even though his sons were now in charge.

It's the satisfaction of being able to make things with real skill – the reward of daily practice – that enables old crocks to keep turning, to the encouragement of us all.

THE BANNING OF IVORY

I'll never forget the time ivory became a banned substance. My work is mostly small and I hadn't bought ivory from merchants for some years. Most of my needs came from bits and pieces of old stuff an antique dealer friend used to keep an eye open for. But for two months I found myself without real work and knew what it felt like to be put out to grass. In theory, of course, you could take advantage of the situation by making works of art that you'd promised to make if you ever found time. In reality, such works are usually made by busy people who make time for them. All my best work has been done in busy times, never in spare time – if there is such a thing.

After a few anxious days, small orders filtered through and kept me going, as they always have done. I make quite a few organ drawstop knobs, thumb pistons and bushes in various woods and plastics, and replacements for ancient organs in ancient ivory. Boxwood and ebony chess sets are always wanted, when I can fit them in.

INTRICATE WORK

Works of art, on the rare occasions when they do appear, are when something superb turns up in the form of an old specimen or picture that gives me an idea to adapt or copy.

The best shapes have usually been done before, but so many haven't been seen for years and are waiting to be remembered by those who are looking for them. Many are designs that can be modified and even improved. If complete originality is insisted upon, the results can be curiously unattractive, unless you happen to be gifted beyond we ordinary mortals.

When such pieces were shown to my grand-father, Lewis Jones (1850–1914), shown here properly dressed, complete with armrest, he'd either say, 'Very nice old cock, but can you earn a living at it?', or, 'That and tuppence (or whatever the current price was) will get you a pint anywhere.'

Lewis Jones (1850–1914).

Not being an arty turner, I'm happier doing a run of repetition work, because every tool movement becomes precise and pleasurable without having to strain the brain. When I've had a surfeit of that, I'm happy to spend time on more intricate jobs, such as the following small repair.

'MIRACLE' REPAIR

The order simply stated: 'Please perform one of your miracles. Thank you.' This man thinks I'm a marvel, I thought, and as I don't like to disap-point him, I'll jolly well have to be one, although he has more faith in my ability than I have.

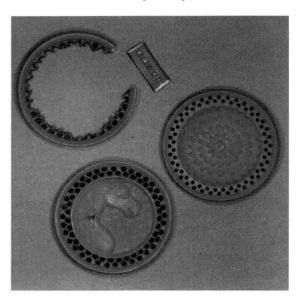

Broken ivory backgammon counter:
before and after.

The order was for an ivory backgammon/ chess counter. I had to make a new rim to screw on the centre portion. At the screwed part, the recessed rim was only ¹⁄₁₆in (2mm) wide and there was nothing to grip in a self-centring chuck, so that a chaser could be used on the middle part.

I clamped a piece of boxwood slightly bigger than the counter in a three-jaw chuck and recessed it so it barely received the counter. The centre portion and the new rim can be seen at the top of the photo above.

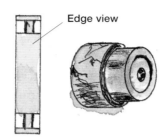

Edge view

Side view of backgammon counter.

A clever friend from the Society of Ornamental Turners, Paul Fletcher, sent me a gadget a year ago which he knew I'd find useful some day. It was simply a tiny ball race with cork glued on one side. Fitting over the back centre, it was perfect to be brought up to support my counter, which had a horse carved in relief upon it. I got the counter running true, and with a ⅛in (3mm) round nose tool, cleaned it up for cutting the screw.

Taking my nicely sharpened, 32 outside chaser with the rosewood handle, and with the tee rest nearly ¾in (18mm) from the work, I set the lathe in motion by foot pedal, very slowly – about 100rpm.

Counter with thread chased.

With my delicate circular movements and no pressure, I struck up a true thread, slightly tapered, to a millimetre or so past the centre, finishing by making a tiny shoulder with the triangular point tool, for the rim to screw up to.

The rim came from my collection of old ivory rings of all shapes and sizes, stored away over the last 100 years, for no ivory is ever discarded. Fixing a suitable one in the four-jaw, I turned a recess roughly to size, opened it with an inside tool, and cut a 32 thread.

After some careful fitting, I decided it didn't want to go on true, so I returned it to store and selected another. It's a better man than me that gets everything right first time.

This time it screwed on perfectly, so I turned the precise recess, perfected the outside of the rim and cut it off. Reversing it in the chuck, I turned the matching recess the other side,

then turned down the unwanted male threads on the counter.

I made sure the rim could be screwed on and off reasonably well, without being too loose or too tight because, on repairs of this sort, the rim has to be stained to match the middle before it is finally tightened home with a dab of glue.

Next, I fixed the rim alone in the outside jaws of a little three-jaw, on the Holtz. If the middle steps of these jaws are used, no bruising occurs. I drilled two rows of 36 holes, using a drill spindle and the division plate and index.

And that was it. I sent it to my client, who stained it to a very good match. The middle part, where the threads had been turned down, he stained with a matching fibre-tipped pen.

The holes were a shade smaller than the originals in the set, but these counters are often banged down on the table by thoughtless players, so it was prudent not to weaken the fragile rim by further enlarging the holes.

KEEP TOOLS SHARP

I've turned 1,500 braille erasers in the last couple of months. They are made from casein rods which are soaked in a bath, so they turn beautifully while I enjoy selected LPs. These concentrate the mind and prevent boredom that would otherwise intermittently hold up production.

Casein braille eraser.

My two main tools are old files, and they keep their edge as well as HSS, and cut nicer. Such tools are oft referred to as scrapers, but not by me. It is people who are scrapers, not tools. My tools turn shavings, not dust, because I don't choose to scrape with them.

I've seen gouges and chisels used as scrapers by some who have a reputation for not using so-called scrapers unless unavoidable. When father says turn, let us all turn, not scrape, with suitable tools which shouldn't be insulted by giving them derogatory names.

The great three square file I use as a ½in (13mm) round tool, once 1ft (3.6m) long, has worn down to about 2½in (64mm) and has a long handle to compensate. I sharpen it carefully, so it will last a few years yet. I grind it as little as possible, and never to the very edge, which I keep sharp on the medium India stone, using the movement as illustrated below, swinging the handle like a metronome, following the contour of the edge, but without any force. If I don't allow it to become blunt I can bring the edge sharp with a few rubs.

Round tool – my worn down old warrior.

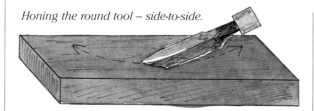

Honing the round tool – side-to-side.

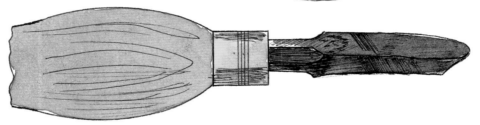

Now, Bertram never sharpened his round tools and gouges like that, but used the narrow edge of the stone, which developed a deep groove and gave him what he wanted. I don't think either way is superior, it's just what you get used to and that's all there is to it.

The other vital weapon

Honing the round tool – using a groove on the edge.

is the square tool – another worn down old flat file which needs a long handle now it's so short. It has a 45° bevel for front and side. I need the side to turn a perfect tip on the eraser, and I used to use a favourite Washita stone I bought at Gamages in Holborn, one of the finest of the emporia soulless man ever had the stupidity to replace with offices 20 years ago. True, the stone was a corner missing and it had been worn hollow, but it was still good. It should be, it cost me 12 bob.

Worn down old flat-file square tool.

SHARPENING STONES

I trued it some time ago because when you start with a flat stone, you fondly imagine it is still fairly flat, even after years. It's not until you hold it to the light with a straight edge that you realise the harm you may have been doing to tools.

Another thing you forget, if indeed you knew in the first place, is how easy it is to flatten your good old stone again – we all dodge work.

Now, when you discard an old cooker with its glass door, hang on to that sheet of glass because that's your surface plate for truing your stone. All you need is half a teaspoonful of fine grinding paste thinned with paraffin (kerosene), used gradually, and you should get your stone nice and flat in 5–10 minutes. You'll wonder why you didn't do it long before. And what a lovely feeling as you sharpen your tools on something dead flat that cuts.

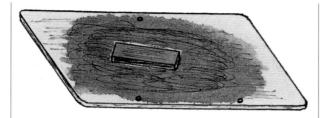

Oven glass and grinding paste for restoring worn oilstone.

FAVOURITE TOOLS

Unfortunately I had that stone stolen. I kept it in its beech box, tightened in a small vice just at the right height. The stone was 'lifted', leaving the box. I have another old Washita stone, but it's not as good.

Sometimes I wonder if it's 'all in the mind', when we think of tools we like to use. Perhaps I haven't made friends with this stone yet, but it is a fact that some tools from the same source will be excellent and others poor in comparison. Of course I have a number of square tools, round tools, etc., and certain ones become favourites for specific jobs.

Honing a square tool should be done delicately, especially at first. After a rub on the top surface, place the bevel down on the stone and feel for the whole surface of the bevel to make positive contact all over as you lightly move the tool to and fro.

Examine it to see if you are placing uneven pressure on one side. It's a skill you need to develop, as in flat filing. It does make a difference when you can put a good edge on a tool.

Files, like cutting tools, are a mixed bag. Some are useless, others fair, and some very good, but I have found HSS tools are the same, which can be upsetting when you've paid a lot for it – including VAT. I've just bought a ½in (13mm) skew which cuts like mild steel – fools and their money . . . !

Mild steel is quite suitable for armrests which support another tool, and do not have to cut. The way I make them is from ¼in (6mm) round steel. I heat the end cherry red, flatten it moderately with a hammer and turn the end up by fixing it in the vice and hammering it over. The surfaces are then filed smooth and rubbed over with the oilstone. The handle should be a foot (300mm) long and the steel should protrude about 6in (152mm). With this essential tool, I don't have to fool about swivelling my tee rest every two minutes. And, do you know, I have never seen an armrest for sale, neither have I known anyone who bought a special piece of steel to make one.

Almost every junk box will have something that can be utilized – a length of mild steel, round or flat, or a long bolt; it doesn't matter. But if you find it doesn't work, don't blame the armrest. Think of Bruce and the spider! You'll get there in the end.

Armrest.

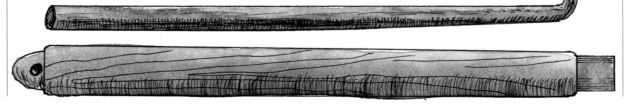

Chapter 4
Lidded, Inlaid BOX

F riday, 15 April, '94: Not a fine day, but could have been a lot worse. I'm up early because at 7.15am I set off with a couple of pals to the Midlands Woodworking and Woodturning Exhibition at Stoneleigh Park in 'Willie the Shake's' own county of leafy Warwickshire.

Not having been in that area for half a century, I wondered vaguely if it'd be anywhere near glorious Honily, an airfield where I spent the happiest five months of my life in '43, on a small detachment from 116 Squadron, as an engine fitter.

There was only a handful of us, and when we weren't slogging away looking after some Oxfords, we'd be playing solo at a ha'penny, penny and three ha'pence and cycling around the delightful sleepy villages of Chadwick End, Hockley Heath, Knowle (where the famous Edwardian Lady came from), Lapworth, Tile Hill etc., singing – and sometimes dancing – in some of the finest little pubs in this favourite county of mine.

Should any of my old campaigners read this, I hope they'll drop me a line. I was also known (by some) as 'the golden voice of Oxygen', later on, when I was attached to 422 AFAP.

I didn't recognize anything at Stoneleigh, but it was an excellent little show with plenty of lathes working, including a pole lathe.

Reg Sherwin was demonstrating on a Poolewood lathe, and he turned for me one of his magnum goblets, only $\frac{3}{16}$in (4mm), for which he keeps a set of tiny tools in a special wallet. I wondered where on earth to put it for safety, but Reg was used to this problem – he provided me with a full-size plastic shopping bag.

That fine turner Keith Rowley, who was doing encouraging work on a Myford Mystro, made me very welcome. A young lad was achieving some fair old gouge work under Keith's watchful eye.

I USUALLY find that if there's a wrong way to do a thing I do it

Reg Slack and Roy Sutton looked as if they'd just stepped out of their most excellent videos. Even my good friend Stan King of Epping was there, and joined us for a cuppa with his friend.

I was Tannoyed by Reg Sherwin to give information on bone lace bobbins to an enquirer who had enjoyed my articles, but found that the ordinary fixed or revolving back centre

Left *Screwed box with ivory inlay, decorated with ECF.*

tended to split the bone. I advised the use of a hollow quill centre, shaping the end of the bone to a point and, of course, reiterating the most essential – to boil the bones and keep them moist.

There were tools and materials of all varieties and prices. Even the impecunious could take home something. I took home a couple of vernier callipers and a depth gauge for £10 the three.

A set of full-size, handled woodturning tools for a tenner might not prove terribly efficacious, but for all I know they may cut quite well. (I did *not* buy those.)

COMBINATION CHUCK

For some time I've been considering a combination chuck. Why? In case I need one some day. In order to keep abreast of current trends. But mostly because I can resist anything but temptation, as Oscar said.

I took advantage of Craft Supplies' show offer of a 2000 Precision Combination chuck. They promised to send the body to fit my Acorn capstan head, which is 1½in (38mm) x 8 teeth per inch. I even bought some timber from my friends at the Leigh Timber Company.

The body arrived the following Thursday. Would it fit? It did, except for ¼in (6mm), which wasn't good enough. I set it dead accurately in the outside jaws of the four-jaw chuck and ran my No. 8 inside chaser down it, on the armrest.

The beginning threads were fine, it just needed clearing a little at the end and it screwed home perfectly. But I usually find that if there's a wrong way to do a thing I do it.

TURNING A LIDDED BOX

I assembled the screw point chuck and fixed thereto a small bowl blank, 4 x 2½in (100 x 63mm), after boring the requisite hole. It went on stiffly and, when nearly home, the screw worked loose and I had to take the thing to

pieces, grip the morse tapered, screw-holding contrivance in the vice to unscrew the blankety blank, and whang the darned thing in harder, an error I trust I shall not be guilty of again.

The next mistake I found was in selecting for my lidded box a piece of zebrano, because of its handsomely striped grain. Not having tried it before, I was disappointed to find I couldn't touch it with any of my numerous gouges – it put me in mind of palm tree wood. The tool I found most suitable was my long-handled, ⅛in (3mm) round nose, touched up on the grindstone little and often.

My usual pattern, turned inside the lid.

I cut the requisite dovetail recess and turned a little of the shape I wanted. Then I removed it from the screw and assembled the appropriate expanding dovetail collet (which wasn't easy first time – nothing in turning is).

It seemed to work all right, with a little adjustment to get it true. I decided to try for a screwed lid for no better reason than an insatiable desire to try my chasers on anything remotely capable of taking a thread without crumbling – too much.

I struck a good thread on the inside of the lid with a No. 20 chaser, turned my usual pattern inside and finished with three grades of abrasives, sanding sealer and wax polish on 0000 steel wool.

After rounding it smoothly, I cut it off, then turned the body, cutting a good thread which fitted the lid pretty well. Hollowing the interior, using the long-handled, ⅛in (3mm) round nose, proved simple indeed.

WORKING WITH ARMRESTS

The efficacy of the armrest as a tool support in awkward places is obvious to all who have

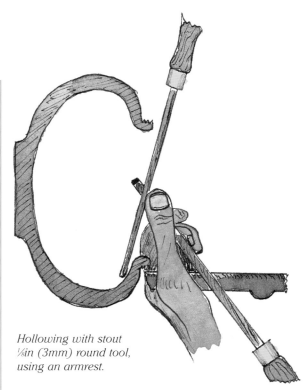

Hollowing with stout ⅛in (3mm) round tool, using an armrest.

used it successfully or watched it in use. The left thumb holds the tool down on the armrest, which firmly controls both the position and manipulation of the tool by the movement of the body and the left shoulder. The upper arm grips the armrest handle and moves the tool exactly where you want it, with the requisite pressure. When the armrest says 'Come along,' the tool has to come. If that sounds familiar you must have read *Coot Club* by Arthur Ransome.

ALTERNATIVE IVORY INLAY

After finishing, I screwed the lid on firmly and turned it slightly domed, then cut a recess in the top, ⅛in (3mm) deep, for an inlaid ring of alternative ivory, about 2¼in (55mm) outside diameter and ⅞in (23mm) inside diameter.

I gripped the alternative ivory in the outside jaws of the four-jaw and turned a ring to fit the recess exactly, by careful use of the vernier calliper. It doesn't matter how many times you have to try it before it fits, just don't make it too small by rushing it.

I applied Araldite and left it to set. It looked quite effective when turned (very slightly domed on the ring) and buff polished.

TURNING BARLEYCORN PATTERNS

I decided to transfer the lid to the Holtzapffel 'Eldorado' lathe, so I cut a matching thread on a spare piece of boxwood and clamped it in a three-jaw, where it ran as true as a die. My aim was to make a barleycorn pattern upon the alternative ivory ring using the eccentric cutter and the 144 circle on the division plate.

To ensure the barleycorns don't have their sides mutilated, the instrument must be given a setting which will result in touching circles all around the work. The Rev. G. A. Grace devised a contrivance to achieve this in the shape of a faceplate or chuck faced with white material, about 4in (100mm) in diameter, which fits on the mandrel nose. Radial lines are marked upon it. To obtain touching circles, their number must be divisible into the chosen circle of holes on the division plate – in this case 144.

With the aid of the indicator, the tool in the eccentric cutter can be set in accordance with the space available – the inlaid alternative ivory ring. To make the indicator, I had a faceplate of white casein about ⅜in (10mm) thick and 4½in (115mm) in diameter, which I turned to a flat surface.

Zebrano powder bowl, lid inlaid with polyester resin.

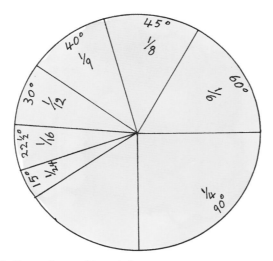

Indicator for touching circles.

With a pointed tool in the ornamental slide rest, it was traversed from the centre to the circumference, with enough penetration to leave a fine line on the face of the indicator.

Using the 144 circle, lines were scribed at one-quarter (36 holes), one-sixth (24 holes), one-eighth (18 holes), one-ninth (16 holes), one-twelfth (12 holes), one-sixteenth (nine holes) and one-twenty-fourth (six holes), all of which are aliquot divisions of the 144 circle on the division plate. The lines were then inked in and, when dry, faced off a trifling amount to remove surplus ink.

The lid is in the chuck. The eccentric cutter (in the slide rest) is placed in front of the work,

and the tool given eccentricity and radius commensurate with the position and width of the alternative ivory ring. This is a rough setting. The slide rest is then moved back, without lateral displacement, to enable the work to be removed and replaced by the indicator.

A pair of lines on the indicator which more nearly coincide with the present tool setting turns out to be one-eighth of the circle. This is found by bringing up the eccentric cutter, with its double angle tool in it, close to the indicator.

The point of the tool is adjusted to swing just up to or down to any pair of adjacent lines. This is done by looking along the upper line selected and turning the indicator round until the point of the tool is directly opposite the line.

The tool is then turned downward and should meet the lower line exactly. If it doesn't, it can be made to do so by adjusting the radius.

As we're cutting on a narrow ring, we haven't much to play with, but the one-eighth was very close and the tool was tightened in the eccentric cutter, the slide rest carefully withdrawn without lateral displacement, and the indicator was replaced by the chuck, with lid clamped in it. Bringing the slide rest up to the work again, the setting is correct for a pattern which requires touching circles.

All we need now is a suitable sequence of cuts for eight sets of barleycorns, having regard to the fact that the greater the number of holes passed over in the dividing, the larger the resulting barleycorns.

This is most desirable, but it means deeper cutting in order to bring the corns to an apex. The plan angle of the tool is a bit less than 120°, but I must say I don't strain my brain by being over technical. I usually go by experience, trial and error.

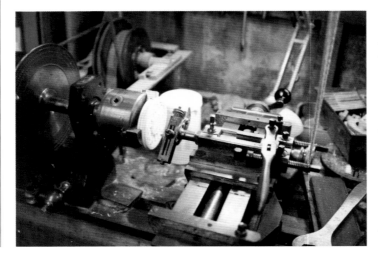

Eccentric cutter in position
(but on another job).

To observe whether the tool has brought the barleycorns to an apex, I pencil over the parts where the pattern is to be made, then the cutting out of the pencilling will indicate whether or not the corns have an apex.

I do three things before starting the actual cutting:

1 Test to confirm that the circles touch, by setting the index at 144 and making a shallow circle, then advance the index to the eighteenth hole (one-eighth) and make another circle. If the circles don't exactly touch, all you need to do is to increase or decrease the tool's radius.

2 Sharpen the tool to its correct angles in the goneostat, on a fine Arkansas stone, without disturbing the radius.

3 Devise a pattern of eight sets of barleycorns. Here is my sequence, arrived at by dividing 144 by 8 and making three small and three large advances in each sequence of 18, viz, 2, 4, 6, 10, 14, 18/20, 22, 24, 28, 32, 36/38, 40, 42, 46, 50, 54/56, 58, 60, 64, 68, 72/74, 76, 78, 82, 86, 90/92, 94, 96, 100, 104, 108/110, 112, 114, 118, 122, 126/128, 130, 132, 136, 140, 144.

Two boxes with six-set barleycorn pattern.

A favourite pattern, when space is not so limited, is a series of six sets of barleycorns, still on the 144 circle, 2, 4, 6, 12, 18, 24/26, 28, 30, 36, 42, 48/50, 52, 54, 60, 66, 72/74, 76, 78, 84, 90, 96/98, 100, 102, 108, 114, 120/122, 124, 126, 132, 138, 144. This pattern can be seen in the photo below.

Should the finish be less clean and sparkling than you would wish, remove the tool and re-sharpen on the Arkansas, ending by rubbing the face to ensure a clean edge.

Replace the tool exactly as it was, pushing it up to the depth stop in its last circular cut, and tighten it. Then, easing the depth stop back a fraction (little more than a whisker) go over the whole pattern again, and that should give it sparkle.

It must be said that nothing sparkles like ivory, but when we have to use man-made alternatives, perhaps a little assistance may be permitted – toothpaste on a soft brush.

Ornamental cuts aren't meant to be polished because the edges would be marred. The tools themselves, when superbly 'got up', as G. A. Grace used to say, impart their own polish, but I am not an ornamental turning purist, you understand, and do as I please.

For those to whom the foregoing is esoteric balderdash, keep it handy in case someone leaves you an ornamental turning outfit in their will. Or, if an absolute beginner, just enjoy cutting whatever regular patterns you fancy, without worrying about barleycorns, until you are accustomed to completing patterns without error.

For small patterns, it is unnecessary to bother with touching circles, and by experience you can get barleycorns on small patterns. Don't let it bother you if they are mutilated, because patterns are always handsome and nobody is going to remark on it.

I never criticize the work of others. Half the time it's better than mine anyway, and the artist's intention is his or her own business.

Of course, I might have guessed my screw on the zebrano box was double-useless because it warped slightly oval in a few days. I simply replaced the body in my combination chuck and turned down the threads, so the lid fits loosely like m'lady's powder bowl.

Chapter 5 ● Turning *Alternative* IVORY

I was pleased to see that alternative ivory, tortoiseshell, horn, wood etc., is now being offered in small quantities in *Woodturning*, as more turners will have the chance to try it for themselves.

It is a fraction of the cost of the real thing – if you could get the real thing. Alternative ivory is fine to turn if certain rules are observed.

Number one is, it is rather fragile and you mustn't make a habit of dropping it. However, fine china is extremely popular, in spite of its vulnerability, and alternative ivory isn't as fragile as that. Delicate or slender pieces must be treated with care, but solid items, boxes, inlays, embellishments to wood turnery, etc., are reasonably tough.

ORGAN DRAWSTOP KNOBS

To lessen the difficulties the woodturner might have in trying such a different material, I'll take you through the process of making two-piece organ drawstop knobs, then you'll be fully

equipped to handle it, if not painlessly, at least with understanding.

The organ stops could be made solid, of course, but it simply isn't done in the 'hardwood and ivory' fraternity (or sorority) as it would be no quicker and terribly wasteful. There are eight stages, including buff polishing.

STAGE ONE – CUTTING THE BLANKS

Cut the 1⅛in (31mm) rod into short lengths for the three- or four-jaw, self-centring chuck, then, with a narrow parting tool (which I call a screever), about ¾₄in (1mm) thick, cut off the

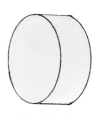

Head blank.

requisite number. Even here you can spoil a piece by a clumsy cut that leaves a hole in one side. If, in spite of care I still find trouble, I complete the cut with a coping saw.

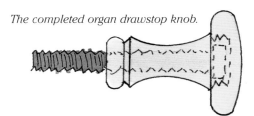

The completed organ drawstop knob.

Left A 'deer' friend carved in the fifties.

Side and plan views of the screever.

Next, I fix my 3in (75mm) Velcro sanding disc in the three-jaw and ensure the outer side of the organ stop head is perfect, so that when turned to a dome, there will be no blemishes to show up under the engraver's colour.

STAGE TWO – TAPPING THE THREAD

Each piece is centred in the three- or four-jaw, surfaced, and countersunk with the side of the splendid square tool. A flat-bottomed hole is made and tapped!

It's deceptively simple, but so easily muffed that when first I did them in ivory, I wrote out a full page, step-by-step guide, as a spoilt ivory head is a fiver down the drain.

Square tool.

This is what I wrote in a notebook entitled, *A Gallimaufrey of tips and wheezes – O.K. and obsolete*. Tapping ¼in BSP – this curious old thread is actually ½in (12mm) diameter, 19 teeth per inch.

'Drill shallow hole with a spear drill – about ¼in (6mm) – and open with small inside tool. Make flat-bottomed hole with ⁷⁄₁₆in (11mm) D-bit.

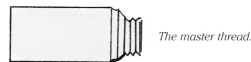

The master thread.

'Turn an annular recess in the bottom of the hole with special tool. Countersink the opening a trifle. Start thread with a 19 inside chaser on the armrest, fairly deeply, but begin very lightly to allow it to cut a true thread.

'If you slant it in with a delicate touch you'll very likely get a true thread. If not – and one doesn't always – go in with the tap (in a tap wrench), dipping it in water first, and pulling the lathe round by hand.

'You will feel when to stop, obviously. The use of the chaser first is to give the tap a lead in, because it's very easy to strip on shallow holes.

'If you find the tap won't start, don't force it, but have another try with the chaser before trying the tap again. Try the master thread for fit.'

Alternative ivory should be treated with the same care, as it can strip easily, but it's a strong thread nevertheless. A touch of the round tool alongside the thread, but leaving the full required diameter, completes stage two. But be sure the opening is countersunk.

STAGE THREE – TURNING THE HEADS

Fix an adapter plug (which could be the master thread) in the three-jaw and turn the heads with

Small, quarter-round tool.

Inside tool (three square file)

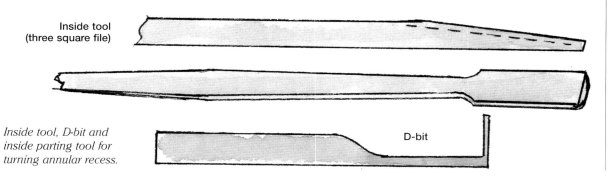

Inside tool, D-bit and inside parting tool for turning annular recess.

Head – tapped and countersunk.

D-bit

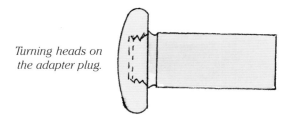

Turning heads on the adapter plug.

round tool and square tool. I use a small, quarter-round tool for the back, but the ordinary round nose will do. Finish the front impeccably, with three grades of abrasive paper.

STAGE FOUR – PARTING OFF

Using ¾in (20mm) rod, cut off the required number, allowing ⅜in (10mm) for the thread. I always skim the rod, as the outside is often uneven.

STAGE FIVE – TURNING THE SHANK

Grip the thread end in the three-jaw firmly, and turn the shank to finished perfection, except for the last few millimetres next to the thread. Also drill the hole for the cheese-headed screw that passes right through the shank in this particular knob. Don't drill right through, as it could break out disastrously.

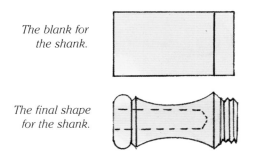

The blank for the shank.

The final shape for the shank.

What tools are best for turning alternative ivory? I know many woodturners are able to work with a modest number of tools which do all they require. I do admire them. I'm quite different. I keep an assortment which, if I take it with me for demos, I usually get someone strong to carry.

Gouges and skews are out for alternative ivory, which shatters under the onslaught. A ⅜–½in (10–13mm) round tool is fine, applied astonishingly lightly and well sloped down as illustrated below.

The gap between tee rest and work allows the essential freedom of movement. Remember also, the left hand should be below the tool rest, never on top of the tool.

The grinding angle is similar to that required for brass turning. I don't actually measure angles myself as a rule, I just try them and find what works best.

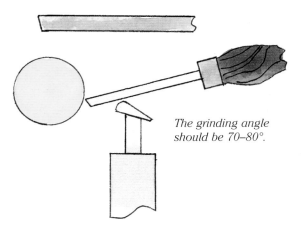

The grinding angle should be 70–80°.

I may pick up my ½in (13mm) HSS Sorby round nose and find it cuts well. If it seems a bit fierce – which it sometimes is – I change to a lighter round tool made from an 8in (203mm) half-round file and this does much better.

YOU WILL soon learn the material's limitations and enjoy turning it

As the tool is applied, do not put pressure on it at all. Traverse along the work in a dragging cut until you get good fat shavings. When these are consistent, you have the measure of the material and can then turn more confidently.

Too much pressure may cause bits to break out, but you will soon learn the material's limitations and enjoy turning it. Tools may be used with fiercer grinding angles, but polyester is not kind to these and soon dulls them. That's why I like to keep spares handy, so I don't have to keep stopping to sharpen.

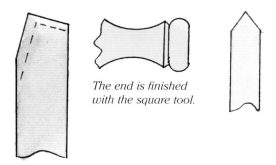

The end is finished with the square tool.

Until you become accustomed to the nature of the beast, you may do shattering work, so the rule is, exercise delicacy at all times. Incidentally, this is also the rule for screw-cutting. You can only put the pressure on when your reflexes are sufficiently educated. With alternative ivory this calls for a lot of finesse.

The end of the shank can be finished with the square tool, although for these I normally use a flat point tool, as I never use one tool if I can use two or three. We all have personal idiosyncrasies.

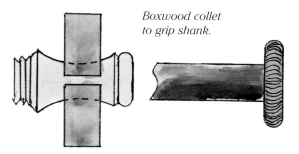

Boxwood collet to grip shank.

STAGE SIX – SCREWING SHANK TO HEAD

All we have to do now, is join the two parts together by screwing the shank to the head. I like stage six best of all.

From my metal box of boxwood two-piece collets, I select one that matches the shanks. You simply turn the appropriate hole in the turned boxwood (or other hardwood) and saw it in halves.

Placing the shank within it, it is gripped in the four-jaw and encouraged to run more or less dead true by tapping the collet – never tap the alternative ivory.

I used a three-jaw for years, although you cannot get such accuracy with three jaws on a two-piece collet as you can with four jaws which, of course, grip evenly.

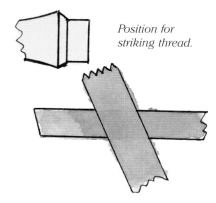

Position for striking thread.

Turn the portion to be threaded down, leaving it oversize, then cut the counterpart of the countersink in the head with a small oblique tool. I made mine from a three square file 40 years ago and cut a quick spiral on the handle with a rounded cutter, in an idle moment, making it at least one tool I can positively identify among the shavings.

In cutting the thread, you need to apply the chaser about 8 o'clock as lightly as a feather, travelling to the left at the proper rate of traverse.

Once a thread is cut, it's merely a matter of retaining some thread as you turn and chase it down to the good fit you want, using the square tool alternately with the chaser.

Easier said than done? Let's have a go! For practice, grip a small length of alternative ivory or hardwood in the self-centring chuck and start

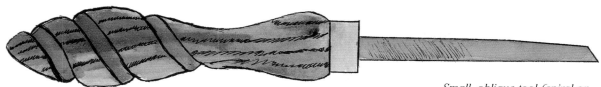

Small, oblique tool (spiral on handle made with round cutter).

the lathe. Anything up to 400rpm will do, and if your lathe speed happens to be a bit higher, we'll accept that because we can't do much else.

With the tee ½–¾in (12–20mm) from the work, move your sharp chaser along to the left, at the extreme end of the rod, having it sloping well down and using no pressure at all.

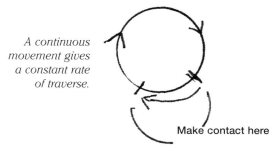

A continuous movement gives a constant rate of traverse.

Make contact here

I make little circles in the air with the end of the tool and make contact with the work as the chaser moves to the left, at the bottom of its circle, as shown above. Keep it moving, because if you stop when it is touching the rod – if only for a second – you'll get a series of useless rings.

After some practice, you will not only cut a thread, but will have learnt the correct rate of traverse needed to obtain a true thread. There's nothing academic about it, just the knack. As old Bertram used to say when tackling something new, 'Some other fool can do it, and so can I!'

A coarse thread requires a faster rate of traverse than a fine one, and likewise, a large diameter needs a slower rate of traverse than a small diameter, hence the need to practise, especially if you're using expensive stuff.

When you're confident, you are ready to try your actual workpiece. Having cut a thread, it will usually be too big. Turn it down a little, leaving enough thread to guide your next

chasing, and you should get a perfect fit with the head.

The countersunk mating is of two-fold value: first, it beds down accurately and, second, it prevents having a wafer-thin and crumbly mating surface on the shank, which is vulnerable to shock.

Before removing the shank, I take the spear drill and meet the hole already drilled from t'other end. Then I turn out the top to accept the cheese head of the screw.

STAGE SEVEN – FINAL SHAPING

Wrap two thicknesses of narrow abrasive paper around the head, and fix in the three-jaw circumspectly, i.e., not tight enough to damage and not loose enough to fly out when you move in with your sharp, ½in (12mm) round tool. Not the heavy one, but the light half-round file one.

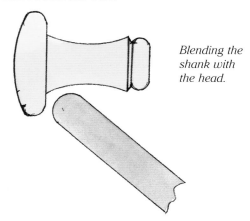

Blending the shank with the head.

With the tee well back, at least 1in (25mm), and using the armrest, lightly, allow the round tool – well sloped down – to blend the shank in with the head, until all you see is a delicate line where the join is.

33

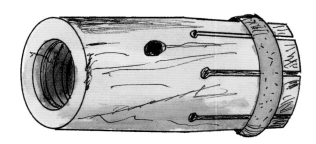

Alternatives: boxwood spring chuck or split collet.

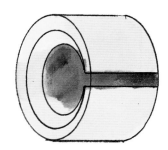

STAGE EIGHT – FINISHING

A very low speed is required as you paper it without any pressure, for that would easily dislodge the knob, with almost certain damage. Now, I must tell you that I can get away with this because of my foot-controlled variable speed – plus experience. The safer method would be to use a boxwood spring chuck or a split collet in the three-jaw, which holds more firmly and doesn't endanger the work or the worker.

I've written this often, but *never* use your jaw chucks until you've filed, ground and stoned all the sharp leading edges and corners, so that they can't easily lacerate. For those who offer their lathes for demonstrators, please see that all sharp jaws are disarmed.

ALTERNATIVE IVORY PECULIARITIES

Of course, as a project for your man in the street, a drawstop knob is a non-starter. Yet, for the purpose of explaining alternative ivory peculiarities it's ideal, and I hope many will be encouraged to obtain some to use as exciting embellishments to their first class woodturnery.

The light and floury shavings are very clinging and need clearing every hour or so, but they are not toxic or unpleasant. When they stick to the work, as they often do in an irritating way, I clear them in an instant with an old toothbrush, applied safely from the rear.

The finishing of alternative ivory is the same as I use for wood. Three grades of abrasive paper, 180, 240, 400 wet-and-dry, followed by 0000 steel wool – with wax if you like. I then polish on the calico buff with Cannings Crown or Lustre compo.

NEVER use your jaw chucks until you've filed, ground and stoned all the sharp leading edges and corners

A friend contacted me recently to say he'd rung Walshes in Clerkenwell, a firm I recommended for polishing compounds. He said, 'I asked for cunning Crown compo but all they could offer was Lustre, at £1.60 a bar, plus £2.50 postage.' I sent him half a bar of mine. Cannings used to have a large emporium at St John Street, Clerkenwell. They're in Birmingham only now, I believe. They used to make Crown and Lustre compos but I never found any difference.

I use it to polish everything, including my nails when I'm putting on the Ritz. I said to my friend. 'You shouldn't begrudge £2.50 post, because it's quite a heavy bar and will last a hobbyist a lifetime! I usually pick up six when I go there!'

A final thought: don't forget a rub of a candle on the tool rest, little and often.

Chapter 6
The POINT TOOL

One of my essential tools is the point tool, made from a three square (or triangular) file. I have evidently failed to make its true shape and function crystal clear, as some readers have only a hazy idea of my exact meaning.

A colleague rang me about it and thought I had the Holtzapffel Volume 4 version in mind. Here's what Holtz says:

'The three sides of the triangular tool, Figs 442 and 443, are ground flat and to a slight curve in the direction of their length; much like the form of a triangular file from which the tool is often made.

'The triangular tool is of about the same dimensions as the graver (440 and 441), the end being also ground off at about the same angle.

'Unlike the graver, the triangular tool cuts almost exclusively by the three angles of its sides or shaft. Sometimes the side edges of its triangular facet are used, but not the extreme point.' Unquote.

Above *Triangular point tool made from round HSS.*

Holtzapffel triangular tool.   *The graver.*

442   443   440   441

The graver and triangular tools are commonly used for hand-turning steel, iron and brass. The point tool I use constantly for hardwoods etc., is quite different. It is ground from a three square file to a three-sided pyramid and used straight from the grinding wheel. The teeth of the file are ground off for 2 or 3in (51 or 76mm), and the corners rounded and smoothed on the oilstone, so it can slide easily upon the tool rest. Only the three cutting edges are used.

SKEW VS POINT TOOL

As you would use a ½in (13mm) skew chisel to surface an end, so you could use the point tool. In this way, small beads or spheres can be turned beautifully without dig-ins.

When cutting a thread up to a shoulder, it is always the point tool I use to cut the shoulder, and sometimes, if I'm making a thread to fit a Chinese chesspiece, I use the point tool as a thread chaser. It has good, sharp angles and works as well as a skew for many jobs where I couldn't use a skew.

The point tool does not appear in Holtzapffel, Evans, Lukin or any other book on turning I've seen – I'm open to correction on this – and if I were to proffer a reason, it would be that professional turners of the last century had no truck with amateurs and not much

with colleagues from another shop. Indeed, it was a closed shop and turners kept their business very much to themselves because of fierce competition.

Apart from gouges, screw tools, twist drills, taps, dies etc., turners made all their own turning tools from whatever steel, files, knitting pins and the like they could pick up. Hardwood and ivory turners didn't use a skew very often because skews do not work on ivory, bone, etc., but the point tool does – *par excellence.*

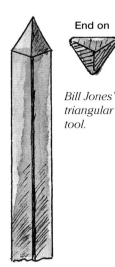

End on

Bill Jones' triangular tool.

It also works on the not-so-hard materials, because it functions exactly the same as a skew, but with none of the proclivities for sliding off in all directions that can spoil a fine and valuable piece of work, just when you thought you had it made. Don't you stand for it.

If you want to make a bead from ³⁄₃₂–⁷⁄₈in (2–22mm) *without* the 'spiral apparatus' – whether you call it your Achilles toe or something not so printable – have the sagacity to use your point tool, because it will be yours from now on or I'm wasting my time.

USING THE POINT TOOL

It's not a scraper and can't be picked up and used first time, just like that. Study its cutting edges and think how the tool must be moved to make that bead.

Obviously, you can't have the tool flat on the tee or you'd be pushing a wedge into the work, but as soon as you tilt it on one of its three corners – any of the three – you push a cutting edge into the work.

After a few minutes' practice on a small

piece of material, you'll realise what a delightful, controllable friend you've got. You won't throw your skew away – of course you won't – but never again will that silly skew leer at you or remind you that he's the boss. Believe me, he'll cringe when you show him your splendid – and cheap – point tool and he'll say, like the dog Moutmorency said (apropos the cat in *Three Men in a Boat*) 'Please don't!'. And when you choose, on occasions, to use him rather than the point tool, he'll be on his best behaviour and you'll find he's a much friendlier fellow because you have shown him he's neither indispensable nor irreplaceable.

The world of amateur turning and its books, for some reason, never discovered the old bone grubber's point tool. They sold vast cabinets of gouges, screw tools, parting tools, chisels and scrapers of all shapes (except the one you *want*), with nary a point tool – except a flat one – in sight.

'MUSEUM' PIECES

I bought one of the Holtz wall cabinets of tools at an auction of the Society of Ornamental Turners 40 years ago. It was mahogany, and contained 75 polished rosewood-handled turning tools. They were shaped as illustrated below, each in a range of sizes. When it was knocked down to me for £9, Fred Howe, the auctioneer, apologized for running me up so high, owing to an out-of-town proxy bidder.

All the tools are quite excellent, but too many are superfluous. In the days when Holtzapffel & Co., flourished and tools could be replaced for a bob or two, I could happily

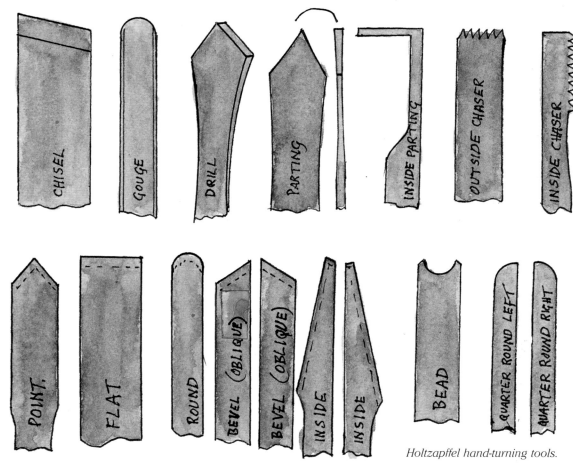

Holtzapffel hand-turning tools.

use some of those tools, but today, when any tool with the Holtz stamp on it is hoarded as a collectors' item, and can change hands at several times the price I paid for the whole cabinet of 75, I use them rarely.

However, this is only because I have most of the tools I want. In other circumstances I'm sure the cabinet could largely fill my needs.

The steel is, of course, excellent and tools of such calibre should be used and enjoyed rather than preserved as collectors' treasures, or relegated to the basement in some mucky museum like a goodly number of very rare ornamental lathes. Society of Ornamental Turners' members are encouraged to shun all museums when seeking to pass on their lathes for whatever reason.

TOOLS of such calibre should be used and enjoyed rather than preserved as collectors' treasures

At the Kensington Science Museum, for instance, some superlative lathes are salted away in a distant store to lie there in perpetuity, beyond the reach or vision of the general public, simply because the wonders of modern science and engineering, whizzing off the assembly lines in ever increasing numbers, demand vital museum space and there is obviously no room for them all.

Yet thoughtless people still bequeath rare and useful machines to museums, fondly imagining they'll be appreciated. They might as well be scrapped for all the fun they'll be allowed to impart to lathe enthusiasts. We must keep antique dealers and passive collectors out and make sure that whoever takes a good ornamental turning lathe is going to use it.

I have a friend who actually owns a Holtz wall cabinet of 64 hand-turning tools that have fluted ivory handles with silver, ornamentally turned ferrules, made for a London exhibition in 1862. I can well imagine him using them too. He has a few high class old lathes, plain and ornamental turning, on which he enjoys making interesting little novelties, all by treadle, because he loves the days and the tools of ancient craftsmen who didn't have motorized tackle.

In a recent letter to me he wrote: 'My two Holtz and several other of my shop tools are foot or hand driven. It is only a hobby – no hurry – good exercise and much more romantic to a historian.'

He has several fine books on horology to his credit and collects and restores ancient horological tools, particularly the tiny lathes known as turns which are driven with a bow in the right hand, while the left does the turning.

In another letter, after reading about my puzzle ball and hammer, he wrote: 'Yup, I gotta immediately make me a magic hammer.' You can tell he ain't a Cockney!

RESTORATION AND REPAIR

A magnificent, three tier ivory and silver 'urn', for want of a more accurate description, came to my shop. It was an ornamental piece and the top tier was missing, having been unaccountably removed by an undiscovered miscreant.

The value of the piece in its present state of incompleteness was negligible. Ergo, anything I could cook up to complete the job would be acceptable, within reason of course.

I had photos of the complete piece and had only two difficulties. First, the two lower tiers were delicately, ornamentally turned with a mysterious pattern the like of which I'd never seen. Something like that shown above right. How the barleycorns were produced intermittently with the fine lines rather stumped me. The very large photos didn't quite reveal the

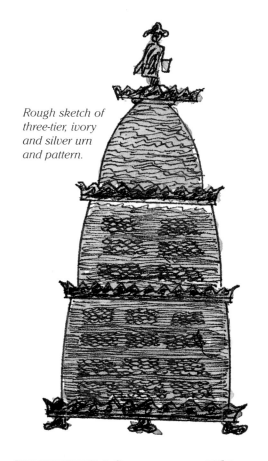

Rough sketch of three-tier, ivory and silver urn and pattern.

Left- and right-pointed quarter-hollow tools, and pattern.

PREPARATION

I'm always pessimistic about work I've never tried, but at least it's safer than being over-confident. I set up a piece of alternative ivory of 2in (50mm) diameter, and started to cut a pattern of delicate cuts. This was achieved by making 28 cuts with a $\frac{5}{32}$in (1.5mm), left-pointed, quarter-hollow tool in the vertical cutting frame for a number of rows.

I then went over the whole lot again with a right-pointed hollow tool, but advanced the dividing by half the distance, so forming a charming, delicate pattern which would not clash with the rest. I sent this sample off for approval and received a prompt OK.

SHAPING, HOLLOWING AND SCREWING

After another three weeks, I made a start with the large ring, which had to screw upon the second tier. The screw was of 18 teeth per inch, 3½in (90mm) in diameter, and fortunately, was hardly warped at all.

It would have been next to impossible to set it up in any chuck, as the other end had a gallery of silver rivetted to it and much cracking of the ivory had occurred.

I had cut a ring from an´old Congo hollow

fine details and the piece was too valuable to risk hiking it around to others who might know.

Second, the large ring and dome I had to replace was of 4in (100mm) diameter, and I doubted whether my meagre stock would run to it. It did, but the ring was an acceptable ¼in (6mm) smaller.

I kept the job for about four months while I frittered the time away with chess, organ work and writing, but soon enough I had to make a start.

Ivory hand saw and slice of ivory.

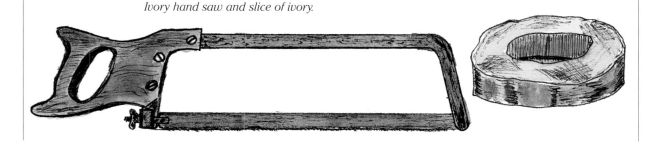

with my trusty, water-lubricated, ivory saw (also from ye famous Society of Ornamental Turners' auctions) and, having pencilled the requisite circle upon it, I hubbed it round to prepare it for the chuck, with my large cutter.

Secure in the outer jaws of the three-jaw, I turned it near the size of the inside thread required, and began to strike the thread with my 18 chaser on the armrest. I'd like to have soaked the ivory first, as it was deuced hard, but it might have impaired the fit when it dried out.

Although wonderfully sound, it was unconscionably resistant to the chaser, which I had to sharpen twice. You can't start a thread with a blunt chaser. I was amazed to find that it screwed on to that old thread absolutely 'smaz-wizzo', as we used to say in 116 Squadron in the happy days.

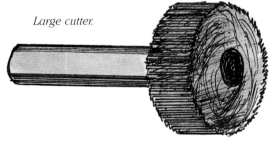

Large cutter.

I reversed it in the chuck, opened it with round and inside tools, and turned a smaller inside thread to take the domed body. There is nothing like those stout outside jaws for gripping positively, without bruising.

By turning and reversing the dome in this chuck, I soon had it shaped, hollowed and screwed most beautifully to the ring – and papered and polished inside with the indispensable Brasso on cotton wool.

I turned and cut an inside thread in the top end while it was screwed firmly into the ring, gripped in the three-jaw. The essence of all this work is the control you have over the lathe speed. When large chunks are zonking round, they can be rather daunting if you can only stop by switching off. You haven't got a third hand, but you've a foot down there doing nothing.

I realize I'm a bit feather-bedded in that respect as, although my workshop space is limited, I have six lathes working, all with variable (foot-controlled) speed.

I'M ALWAYS pessimistic about work I've never tried, but at least it's safer than being over-confident

Many have just one lathe and limited room, and are quite accustomed to their own lathe speed arrangements. Were I in a similar position I would manage just the same, as indeed I have done when demonstrating.

The best work is not done by the turner with the costliest equipment, necessarily, but usually by the one thoroughly at home with his lathe, 'orrible though it may be. And, to make something look easy, you have to work hard.

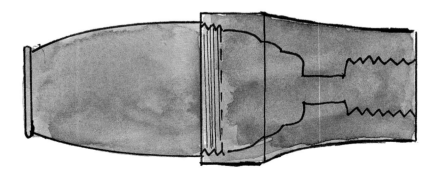

Dome screwed into boxwood cup chuck.

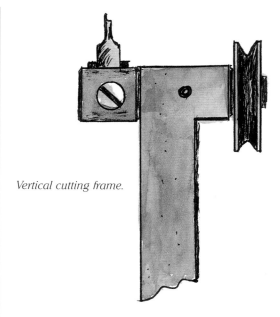

Vertical cutting frame.

DECORATION

Next, I had to set the dome up on my Holtz for the decoration. The more you turn, the more you accumulate, and I found an old boxwood cup chuck and cut an inside thread in it, which, after a little trial and error fitting the dome, got it running true.

I blacked the dome all over with a lead pencil, to reveal exactly when the cuts with the left-pointed quarter hollow tool were deep enough, because the depth had to be increased progressively, as the diameter decreased with the curvature of the dome.

I tightened the left-pointed quarter-hollow tool in the vertical cutting frame and, using the 112 row of holes on the division plate, made 28 cuts at numbers 112, 4, 8, 12 etc.

The ornament results from cutting over every series twice, first with the left-pointed quarter-hollow tool and then with the corresponding right-pointed tool.

I covered the whole dome – an interminable job of more than 1,000 cuts which, non-stop, would take me 90 minutes, with the aid of my home-made automatic counting device.

With several cups of the harmless and necessary, I took quite a bit longer. And I sharpened the tool half way, a tricky job because there is no allowance for error in replacing it exactly.

For each series of 28, the tool is moved to the right exactly its own width, which I found was exactly 10 divisions of the micrometer on the actuating knob of the mainslide.

The shape of the tool causes it to leave 'small portions of the original cylindrical superficies untouched and intermediate to the cuts so far placed upon the work,' as John Jacob instructs.

He continues, (as I did): 'The left- is then replaced by the right-hand quarter-hollow tool, the receptacle of the slide rest traversed back to its original position, and then every series received (28) other cuts, but at intermediate numbers, 2, 6, 10, 14 etc., so that these obliterate the plain portions left by those previously cut.'

To complete the job, I made a smaller dome to screw into that I had just made. This had a tapped hole in the top to take a figurine.

The rest of the work would be done by two marvellous silversmiths making the ornate pierced galleries and the superb carved figure. The ivory was a very fair match, and I gave the decoration a good going over at speed, with Brasso on a toothbrush.

Nobody grumbled at the work because they hadn't expected anyone to be able – or willing – to do it at all.

Subsequently my old friend Paul Fletcher, who specializes in rose engine turning, sent me a sample of the very pattern that mystified me. It was done on the rose engine of course.

The ever-useful Brasso.

Chapter 7 ● *Cabinet* *Knobs* and CAN WASTE

Making cabinet knobs in bone and ivory is a subject I return to because these little knobs are really the only suitable ones for fine pieces of certain types of furniture with small drawers, tool and other chests, davenports, secretaires and the like. If plastic knobs are substituted they stand out like – plastic knobs! The disadvantage of the little plastic knobs is not so much their appearance as their fragility, unless made in an unsuitable and clumsy shape.

Erinoid cord pulls.

I still make knobs in small numbers from time to time, and I do mean small, considering I used to make them by the gross in sizes from ½–¼in (12–32mm) diameter. The largest sold for only about 3/6d or one-sixth of £1, when £1 was worth 50 times its value today – so you can tell how long ago it was.

I've already written how I made them, but few would be able to make them with the same likelihood of success as one who has been geared up for that sort of small screw chasing job for years and has lots of the requisite small chasers (screw tools). But, knowing there are turners who would enjoy producing such things, it struck me that these knobs could easily be done with taps and dies instead of chasers. When I say easily, don't laugh.

We used to start lads of 14 off, before the war when their wage was ten bob a week, and only one in four was successful in using small twist drills and taps in the lathe without smashing them.

The girls, I may add, had a far better record. My sister Dorothy – six years my senior – used to turn erinoid ventilator pulls (known as cord terminals) at the rate of five dozen an hour. I imagine a week would be sufficient for an apt beginner to attain something similar on the hollow mandrel, variable speed, foot-controlled lathe, using just form tool, square tool, two drills and a screever, depending on aptitude of course. It took me longer, I know!

SUITABLE MATERIALS

For those who have progressed in the exceedingly rare skill of using the finest machine tool known to man – I mean the human hand – I can say that with delicacy and care, these delightful knobs and other similar items are begging to be turned from whatever suitable materials you can unearth.

Left *Alternative ivory screwed box, attractively adorned.*

Ivory tusk end (known as 'can waste').

You may ask, why not turn them in the solid? Only if you have far more money than is necessary for normal living. We are using material that would otherwise clutter the place up or be sold for next to nothing.

Bone, of course, does not yield the diameters for solid knobs anyway, and has to be made in two pieces. The tremendous advantage over plastics is the strength which makes a well-made knob last forever.

My ivory knobs, when I'm asked to oblige, come from hollow ends which were designated 'cans' and referred to as 'can waste'.

Much used to be discarded, but not by us, because they came in for swizzle sticks and lace bobbins down to toothpicks. I still retain a fair amount.

CUTTING AND CHUCKING

The heads and shanks are cut as illustrated below, on my 7in (178mm) circular saw. I could hub the head blanks round on the big cutter, but usually I trim the corners off on the saw and fix them in the self-centring chuck so the pencilled circle runs true.

Can sections used for heads and shanks.

Now, when I say true, I mean a turner's true and not a precision engineer's with a DTI (dial test indicator). We accept 'near enough – that's egzackly' – but we often have to work to a thou' in our fitting, and by eye, all without a mike, and we don't get the credit we deserve. And I'm not knocking engineers – they also have their problems, poor things.

I chuck the heads and surface the barkless side, turning with the square tool a small spigot, just enough to grip in the jaws when I reverse it to drill, and tap the barky side, usually turning away most of the bark, though bark on the blind side is quite acceptable.

Heads in self-centring chuck.

If bone is being used it will, of course, be well boiled and kept moist as otherwise, it is too brittle and hard to turn. Drill a flat-bottomed hole with a pilot drill and small inside tool (three square file and don't let 'em tell you different), the requisite diameter for the tap you will use.

Pilot drill and inside tool.

We don't 'chuck and chance it' like a sprog angler, we try everything on a piece of waste first, so that we get the exact diameter: otherwise we'll spoil our ivory.

TAPPING A THREAD

My most common size tap for these is ¼in (6mm) x 26 and I use a drill which accommodates this exactly. Most often we have a small boxwood or horn handle for our taps, but a tap wrench does very well.

Boxwood-handled tap.

Dip the end of the tap in your water pot first, place it accurately in position and, with confidence, push it gently in as you turn the chuck round by hand.

You can see and feel it cutting a thread (or screw), but the completion, when the tap reaches the bottom, may not be so obvious for one to whom this is a new experience, and it may strip. We all do this now and then – I do, but not, I hope, too often. A little more sensitivity and it won't strip.

This, below, is a short length of brass rod or a brass bolt turned down to the correct diameter and threaded with a die. If you find the die doesn't go right up to the shoulder, the thread can be continued by using a single point tool and traversing it along the thread, rotating the chuck by hand.

Brass arbor.

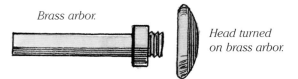

Head turned on brass arbor.

The knob heads can be turned upon this arbor, which is gripped in the three-jaw. To make a pattern of rings on the dome I use a chaser (about 24 teeth per inch), but a point tool will achieve the same result – or you may choose a different pattern.

The rods to make the shanks do not have to be screwed, as they may be turned to a uniform dowel to glue into the furniture. Personally, I usually make them slightly tapered and threaded with a 24 chaser.

The shank is turned something like the illustration above right, but you may prefer your own fancy. It's then gripped in the three-jaw by the dowel, the end turned to the requisite diameter,

and threaded with a die held in a die stock.

The former is secured in the latter by three screws, which are used as adjusters. If the centre screw is tightened while the outer ones are loose, the die is opened to its maximum.

The shank and die stock with die.

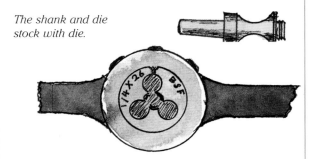

If the thread needs to be a little smaller, the centre screw is loosened and the outer two are fully tightened. If the piece to be threaded is turned accurately to the apposite diameter, and the die is gently and carefully advanced while the lathe is moved round by hand, an excellent thread will surely result.

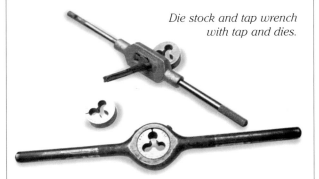

Die stock and tap wrench with tap and dies.

With a point tool the niceties can be completed so that the head screws on in a most satisfying manner. Every time I make a good, well-fitting screw that is neither sloppy nor too tight, even after half a century, I get a

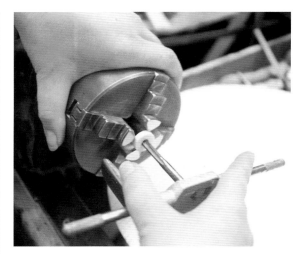

Tap wrench in my daughter Ginette's fair hand.

Ginette using the die.

The tap wrench and die stock in use.

tiny glow of satisfaction. Others may regard it as a disgusting bore, but fortunately, we're not all like Louis Jourdon in Gigi. A fate worse than death.

Polish may be imparted (after fine sanding) by Brasso on cotton wool. I marvel at those who say they can't make two knobs alike. How can they vary if you use callipers, dividers and a modicum of care?

FURTHER USES FOR CAN WASTE

While the cans are out, let me tell you they have other uses. There's one particular job where even old Bill can't use a chaser to cut a thread, and that is in screwing a flag to a chess rook.

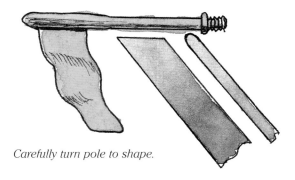

Carefully turn pole to shape.

The rough shape is cut out on the circular saw. My fine, 6in (152mm) saw (foot-controlled variable speed of course) is as versatile as a band saw. I get the flag even more to the shape I want it on the hub – my big cutter.

Then, with the flag sticking through the jaws, I grip it in the three-jaw and get it running true using the back centre. With the armrest, a long, ⅛in (3mm) round tool and a small oblique tool, I carefully turn the pole to shape and finish as much as I dare under the whirling flag.

I turn the end to the exact diameter I need to take the die. Then, withdrawing the tailstock, I cut the thread by easing the die on, turning the chuck by hand. It has to be easy or the slender pole will snap. The rest of the flag is then carved and polished.

DRAGONFLY BROOCHES

Another item I made from hollow cans was these delightful dragonfly brooches, shown below. Butler and Wilson, the famous London jewellery house, used to very much appreciate them.

They are ¼in (6mm) thick, and I used to cut them out complete on my 6in (152mm) circular saw. But one in four snapped in the vice while finishing, so I then made them in two pieces to save material and time.

> EVERY time I make a good, well-fitting screw that is neither sloppy nor too tight, even after half a century, I get a tiny glow of satisfaction

The join is a small ivory dowel, carefully fitted to be invisible when Araldited. The shaping was done with cutters of various shapes, clamped in the three-jaw. Glass cloth and scraping tools achieve a fine finish that yields an immaculate polish on the buff.

I wouldn't expect to take more than an hour each for these, and I'd fix a pin on the back with two 8BA screws. I got a thrill when a top model appeared on the cover of *Vogue* sporting one of my dragonfly brooches.

DEMONSTRATION

On 10 September, I did a day's demo for the Suffolk Mid-Coastal Woodturners at Marlsford. I couldn't have had a better reception or a more enjoyable time.

Peter Taylor had quickly adapted a fine old Drummond round-bed to a BJ variable speed slipping belt job that worked perfectly – so it really can be done.

They wondered why my lathe in the *Woodturning* photo every issue is round the wrong way? It is simply because it is a reflection in the large mirror I have facing me. Ginette took it from behind my right shoulder.

They also said I looked younger and slimmer than that photo. Wow! No wonder I enjoyed my sunny day in delightful Suffolk.

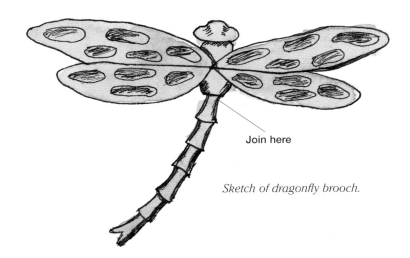

Join here

Sketch of dragonfly brooch.

Chapter 8 ● *Turning* Screwed BOXES

*I*had a challenging little job from John Haywood, who is, among other things, a collector of boxwood boxes of the kind abundant in the last century. It was for a large, screwed, pharmaceutical box which once contained a bottle, but in which someone had made a hole to create a string box.

The rim of the lid was damaged, and John (and I) at first visualized a new top. There was no hurry, but I couldn't see this on my bench without itching to make a start.

John Haywood's broken box.

It didn't take long for me to realize that the 4in (100mm) high golden lid was too good to throw away when, if I could replace just the broken ring, I could kill three birds with one stone.

First, I could retain the handsome-coloured top, which would be difficult to match and a crime to discard. Second, I could use a piece of contrasting wood which would make a virtue of necessity and even enhance the box's appearance.

And, third, I could surprise myself and others if I'd manage to do it. Actually, the idea first occurred when I found a perfect ring of plank-grained blackwood.

THE REPAIRS BEGIN

The first operation was to grip the bottom of the box firmly in the outside jaws of the four-jaw while I ran an outside chaser (screw tool) over the threads. It was 11 threads per inch, measured with my thread gauge.

It's many years since I've been caught out without a chaser the size I want, because I've consistently added to my collection at every opportunity. I found the thread was rather drunk, though strangely, scarcely warped.

After cleaning the thread with the No. 11 chaser, I removed the box from the chuck and

Left Screwed boxwood box, 'not so plainly' plain turned.

clamped in the blackwood ring, which happened to be the perfect size for the job.

With the aid of vernier calliper, armrest, inside tool and 11 chaser, I got that ring to screw perfectly upon the box. The drunken thread passed completely unnoticed, showing that we can worry about trivialities quite unnecessarily.

> # YOU must simply hope for the best and mitigate disaster by experience, fortitude and a sense of humour

Before turning the outside of the ring to shape, I cut a finer inside thread at the top – a 22 teeth per inch thread for the lid to screw into. I began to turn the outside to shape, quite happily, when it suddenly went BANG and jerked out of the chuck.

These jobs are always attended with risk and can't be done at all without it. You must simply hope for the best and mitigate disaster by experience, fortitude and a sense of humour.

JOBBING SALESMAN
That reminds me of Mr Wolfsky, back in the '30s. He was a proper gentleman and Wolfsky was his real name. A stocky 5ft 7in (170cm), he wore fine, city gents' clothes, dark, with pepper and salt trousers, cream spats and a Homburg hat.

With gold-rimmed specs or occasionally a monocle, he looked a bit like Richard Tauber and had a slightly foreign accent. He regarded cigarette smoking without a holder as taboo (it wasn't realized then that fags, among umpteen million other worse things, can kill).

He lived in a suitcase, enjoyed a modest tipple, and was rather a dear old soul who periodically dropped in our De Beauvoir

Town turning shop to beg some saleable items from Bertram. Wolfsky was a jobbing salesman, who carried a case containing choice pieces of craft work he hoped to sell in the city.

He was a high class Burlington Bertie who few would turn away if they could find something for him to buy or sell. You didn't gain much from Mr Wolfsky, but neither were you much out of pocket because of him.

Mr Wolfsky's gavel.

Bertram had an ivory gavel, like the one shown left, which was slightly bruised, having flown out of the chuck as these things do. It happens to everyone. Anyway, Wolfsky snapped it up, like Autolicus, the snapper-upper of unconsidered trifles, and nipped off with it. He returned a week later and paid Bertram, chuckling the while.

'They asked me about the bruise on it,' he said. 'But they took it?' asked Bertram. 'Oh yes,' replied Wolfsky, 'I told them that was where the elephant fell out of a tree!'

He died peacefully – with a valedictory drink I hope – in a hotel bedroom before the war. Where are the Wolfskys of yesteryear? Aye, where are they?

THE REPAIRS CONTINUE
I picked up the box, hardly daring to look. Apart from heavyish jaw marks, everything appeared to be OK. But that bang had tightened the black ring on – permanently, by the feel of things.

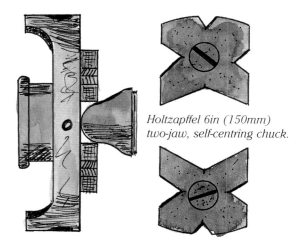

Holtzapffel 6in (150mm) two-jaw, self-centring chuck.

I fixed the box in the chuck, belayed the lathe with a tommy bar, and tried every way with what implements I had, to unscrew it. I don't keep heavy wrenches and the like, because my work is usually small and delicate.

It wouldn't shift. I reversed it, gripping the ring in the chuck. Fortunately there was enough meat on it, otherwise, it would simply have tightened the grip of the screw even more.

I THINK the secret of success is having a sufficiency of oddments of equipment so that, eventually, something is going to work

With 4in (100mm) of stout boxwood to grip, and spit on my hands, I succeeded in unscrewing it in a couple of minutes. Rather a large cup chuck was called for to accommodate the top, which was tapered and shiny. Failing to find one, I fell back on the Holtz 6in (150mm), two-jaw chuck, which is sketched above. These rare little heavyweights have jaws secured by a single screw and can be fitted in four different ways for a variety of jobs, solving many chucking problems. Using the widest vee, the

jaws protruded far enough to grip the sloping top, but to avoid scarring the golden patina I wrapped it in sandpaper – which worked.

I think the secret of success is having a sufficiency of oddments of equipment – not necessarily costly either – so that, eventually, something is going to work.

It's amazing, when repairs and odd jobs come in, how often you find among your stock of chunks of material waste rings from other work (which must *never* be discarded), the exact piece you need.

This used to be a feature of the blacksmith's forge, which was cluttered up to the gunn'ls with all sorts of gubbins. Sometimes we even know where to find the vital piece we know we've got – somewhere!

I cleaned up the broken top gingerly, turned down a spigot about ⅛in (3.5mm) and carefully cut a 22 thread. Working a chaser up to a shoulder when you've only a tiny spigot, makes it essential to reduce speed to 100rpm.

The foot control makes a difficult job easier. I tell you frankly, if it was difficult I doubt if I could do it. I screwed on the ring. It went on alright, but left an unsightly gap on one side.

'Keep going,' I told myself, and cleaned the shoulder a little deeper with my splendid point tool (described in Chapter 7), took another shaving off the thread, blew all the dust etc. violently away, and screwed the ring on again.

NO GLUE

Great heavens, it was perfect, so nice and tight. I spat on my hands again and graunched it up as tightly as I could get it – no glue! A little vee where lid met black and I completed the perfect shape of the ring to match the broken one. The patina on the lid was unimpaired: the chuck marks were polished away on the calico mop with Cannings Crown compo.

My job was presumed to be replacing the whole lid, but as soon as I saw it I realized there was plenty of substance in that lid, which was the nicest part of the box. And the inclusion of the blackwood ring had transformed its appearance.

There was still an unsightly hole in the top and finally I succumbed to the temptation of making a small decorative addition. The hole was the correct size for tapping with a ¼in (6mm), 26 plug tap, and this I did.

Taking a disc of old billiard ball ivory, about 1⅛ x ¼in (28 x 6mm), I drilled and tapped it with the same tap. It's a size I often use for cabinet knobs, and I keep a small brass arbor with the same thread, to support work in a self-centring chuck for turning.

I turned the back first, so that it was slightly dished to match the contour of the lid. Then I reversed it and turned it to the shape shown in the sketch below.

The flower motif I obtained by the use of a couple of Bertram's vee cutters, which he kept on a double-ended arbor of brass, removing one to use the other, if you follow me.

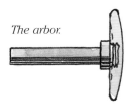
The arbor.

The flower motif.

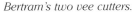
Bertram's two vee cutters.

The cutters set up in the three-jaw revolve at the highest speed you can get (average 2,200rpm on most of the lathes I use). With the disc supported on its arbor, I incised the 12 petals by hand and eye on the thin cutter, following with the broader one, which rounds the petals and the ends too. If you're worried about division plates, pencil the 12 lines in

Box opened, showing re-cut threads.

first, but it makes little difference, truly. With a little practice, the project is quite easy and thoroughly enjoyable.

This incision leaves the surface rather rough, so we smooth it on the flapwheel. A flapwheel is composed of numerous strips of abrasive cloth set in a round rod, which is clamped in the three-jaw. I got mine from Woolworths. It easily papers the petals smooth: and the buff which follows imparts a polished, gem-like perfection quite quickly. A blackwood button with screw is next turned, to secure the flower to the lid. You may use a ¼in (6mm), 26 die if preferred.

Was the job appreciated? 'Absolutely wizard!' said John.

The finished box.

NIGHTMARE

What must be every demonstrator's nightmare is standing, *hors de combat*, at the lathe, in front of an audience which confidently expects the usual effortless efficiency they've come – and most likely paid – to watch.

The lathe being a disaster, for whatever reason, the work flying out of the chuck, the wood disintegrating under the tool, or the unaccountable mishandling of a tool ending in a debacle, are all things that can happen in an exhibition that is risk-oriented beyond question. But, when preparation has reduced the possibility of failure to an absolute minimum, we know it should all go with a swing, don't we? No – we don't!

The fact is, we know only too well that the unaccountable is only too likely to rear its ugly head, hence the nightmares. But still, as a breed we are not normally pessimists, because we can either turn reliably or manifest enough showmanship to handle any normal, or even abnormal, set of circumstances. Further, turners are well aware that mishaps are only too prevalent, and they are naturally sympathetic when a colleague suffers an unfortunate hiccup.

Indeed, should the demonstrator hit snags, it is positively salutary to tyros (who may have imagined such things only happened to them and wouldn't dare assail the 'great ones') to see that 'orrible disasters are in fact common to us all. It reminds me of a recent jaunt my friend and brother, Allan Batty, a superlative professional woodturner and teacher, took me on to Yorkshire and the Lake District.

First, I had a day's demo with the Cumbria Woodturners' Association at Kendal. Allan had arranged everything so there was time aplenty for the preparation I needed. I was using his Union Graduate Variturn, a lathe I'm familiar with, and all went according to plan. I began at 10am, making a screwed box and topping it off with an ivory flower as per the John Haywood box. There was ample time for two more projects and then some 'hands-on' screw cutting for those willing to try. The lathe behaved excellently as did the audience.

The venue was John Page's Kendal Tools and Machinery emporium – a woodturner's paradise. John Page was the perfect host, not only seeing that everything ran like clockwork and keeping us awash with the main necessity, tea, but putting Allan and I up for two days in his glorious Lakeland farmhouse, where Vicki, his wife, made us comfortable.

The Cumbria turners gave us an evening out to remember at Windermere, and after such a meal I spent half the night ruminating – turning in my sleep I call it – and had come up with a Baroque box which I hoped might be as good as I visualised it. It seldom is . . .

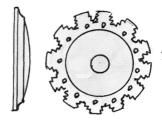

Vandyke cutter – mine is steel, but they may be brass.

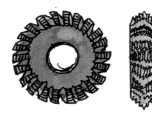

The Vandyke pattern.

For my second day's demo to a different audience, I began by making a Vandyke ivory top for a baroque box with blackboard illustrations showing details of the cutter. This is a cutter I made ages ago and I recommend brass. I made the serrations with a 24 outside chaser, but a flat point tool would have done as well.

Having turned the billiard ball disc nicely domed and dished at the edge, as shown above, I cut 12 Vandykes and then drilled a small hole in each one, after pointing them in with an awl.

I then began the box in my usual way, amusing the audience with semi-serious references to the uncertainty of striking threads by hand chaser.

I must always do this because, although the adept can usually chase threads with facility, the striking of same on the inside of a shallow box lid 'just like that', has got to be a bit of a circus act and I don't know a turner who would argue with that.

Of course, there's no danger involved, hence the buoyancy of my references and, in truth, I do not expect to fail. After all, there is a full ¼in (6mm) on which to strike a 20 teeth per inch thread.

For no reason I could see, I didn't make my usual success. The poet has referred to 'the crisp, smooth truth o' the screw', which I list among my favourite things, but there was nothing crisp, smooth, or truthful about that screw.

SURPRISE

I turned it off and started again with my second 20 chaser (I am a belt and braces man) and to my surprise the result was still uninspiring.

I cut the end off and turned a fresh recess and had another go, but I still couldn't get a crisp screw. A silence had fallen on the proceedings. My word! This was like a Hitchcock film. The suspense was terrible.

Not very hopefully, I finished the inside of the lid and parted it off. Then I turned down a healthy spigot and cut a good 20 outside thread. After several trials I got the lid to fit. But it wouldn't screw home.

By now I was thoroughly demoralised. Fortunately, Allan was sitting in front of me, so I beckoned him out. 'Come and look at this,' I wailed. He did and tried the lid.

'It needs a little off the front,' he said. Of course it did! I turned off ¹⁄₁₆–⅛in (2–3mm) and it screwed home: *not* a very good fit, but I was in the mood to settle for any fit.

I quickly completed my baroque box, sketched below, wishing I'd never dreamt it up in the first place. It looked like the head of a chairman's hammer but, I suppose, none the worse for that. The Vandyked top screwed on with its blackwood button certainly added a recherché touch.

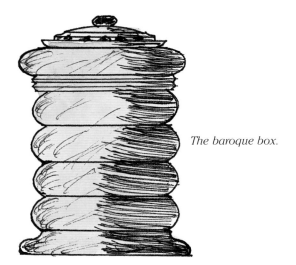

The baroque box.

I'd taken longer than usual on this fiasco, so the break was extended to an early lunch, which completely restored my equanimity and humour. In the afternoon the other two projects went amazingly well, as if to apologize for the morning misery.

Experience is a very fine teacher, 'tis said, and I've thought long and hard about this. In my turning shop I am not stymied when things go awry – I carry on till they go right. I keep in mind what Kipling said about triumph and disaster and endeavour to 'treat those two imposters just the same', thus making a virtue of necessity.

So here's my plan for any future demos – if any! They will be workshop exercises, taking things as they come, the difficulties with the successes. After all, it's unnatural for everything to go perfectly for a whole blooming day, isn't it? Let's have a bit of fun, say I, and 'let come what come may!'.

Chapter 9 ● *Odd Jobs* and Restoration WORK

Several months ago my friend Alan Beecham, that fine turning son of a fine turner to the trade, handed me a partly finished rosewood gun barrel, bristling with screws. The muzzle had a screwed plug in it and the other end, a screwed stopper which also carried inside a screwed cap.

Alan hadn't completed the job, as he thought I might like to experiment and write about it in due course. It was several weeks before I made a start, because the actual puzzle didn't seem to me to be awfully puzzling.

Above *Tiny, carved ivory urns, for 'Lady Jane'.*

Screw guns with a pair of 16 thread chasers.

The muzzle was bored halfway and carried a cannonball. At the front, enclosing the ball, a slotted plug screwed home. The puzzle was to

Screw gun.

 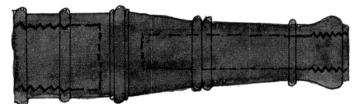

locate the screwdriver within the gun in order to unscrew the plug.

Well, you simply unscrewed the end of the breech. This had a cap screwed on it and when unscrewed the 'screwdriver' was revealed. Oh well, I thought, I'll have a shot at it – ouch!

I made a smaller model in boxwood, sketched below, even studying pictures of cannons to get a realistic shape. The breech end screwed in OK, but a fresh idea came out of the blue that might make the puzzle less of a pushover. Not a lot, but better than the original.

I selected African blackwood for the trial and set down the modus operandi step by step in my usual way, to avoid the necessity of using my brains when I make any more. My blackwood is in square lengths and can be gripped in the four-jaw chuck – length 4in (100mm). The method is reproduced here.

STEP ONE

Turn the piece to a cylinder, then drill a ⅜in (10mm) hole for two-thirds of the length. Cut an inside thread for the muzzle plug. I found 16 teeth per inch about right. Countersink the entrance slightly.

STEP TWO

Reverse and grip by the muzzle end. You can exercise your ingenuity in turning the breech end with its decorative beads. Altho' I draw the shapes first, I don't necessarily follow them religiously, because a flat piece of paper isn't the same as the solid job, and subtle refinements often occur with me.

I could use tiny bead tools which would make an impeccable job, but I prefer to use my faithful three square point tool to make those refinements.

Now, I've been using the said tool for half a century, and the wrist work in its manipulation is as natural and inconsequential as cycling, swimming, or writing. But all those activities have to be learnt: even one of our foremost ornamental turners recently told me he'd made one of my point tools, after reading my enthusiastic comments – and couldn't use it!

I don't suppose I could, when first I clutched one in my tiny fist, but I simply can't remember. When I began, I found *all* tools were unable to give me the results I wanted, and it must've been many weeks before they did.

I can only say that the point tool and the chaser (screw tool) were no more difficult than any other and, like Ashley Iles, as no-one had told me the skew chisel was hard to handle, I had no bother.

The straight bits between the beads were

turned with a honed ⁵⁄₃₂in (3.5mm) parting tool, finishing with a butterfly's wing touch as the tool is moved from side to side, obviating tool marks.

I told the aforementioned ornamental turner that I used three grades of abrasive paper and 0000 steel wool. He was derisive. '400 wet-and-dry?' he chortled, 'I use 3,600.' He told me where to get it too. I told you he was one o' the foremost.

Next (we're still on step 2) I turned a flat-bottomed hole about ²³⁄₃₂in (18mm) in diameter and 1in (25mm) deep, and cut therein a 16 teeth per inch screw. Inside and outside I then finished as above, using wax on the steel wool.

STEP THREE

Reverse in the chuck again. Three methods for chucking are open: a boxwood collet, halved, that fits between the two end beads; a screwed plug, gripped in the four-jaw, upon which the breech end screws; or several thicknesses of abrasive paper, wrapped around the breech end clamped in the chuck, and supporting the muzzle end on the live centre.

I chose the last method, adding a piece of thin leather outside the abrasive paper and not bothering with tailstock support. I then finished turning the gun.

STEP FOUR

Actually, I made several attempts before arriving at this, but, altho' I'm going to alter it yet again, this is the mark two model. A fresh piece of blackwood is fixed in the four-jaw. Next to the breech end, which will be turned to shape later, I turn an oversize spigot, and at the end of that a much smaller spigot, as shown in the sketch below.

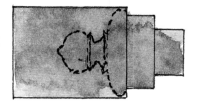

Breech end.

The next step, an idea out of the blue, was to make this end part (upon which the cap is screwed, hiding the screwdriver) a left-hand thread! This would make the puzzle, because it wouldn't be obvious that there was a cap, let alone a removable one, and if anyone thought of trying to unscrew a suspected cap he would hardly twist it clockwise. He'd try unscrewing in the normal way, thus further tightening it. But could I make a left-hand thread?

Usually I have no call for such things, but obviously, if the chaser is traversed to the right instead of left, a left-hand thread should result. And it did.

Slowing the lathe to 100rpm or less – with my slipping belt variable speed controlled by a foot pedal – I dropped the 16 chaser below centre and, starting at the extreme end of the small spigot, where I'd made a deep vee with the point tool, I made a fairly fast, but gentle, traverse to the right, allowing the tool to cut its own thread, as illustrated below.

Traversing to the right for a left-hand thread.

Smaller spigot for screwdriver end.

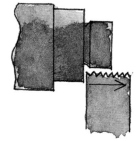

The extreme slow speed of the lathe allowed time to place the chaser precisely back at its beginning for each traverse, which I reckoned went at the rate of about two per second.

I'd allowed a bit for practice, but having cut a good left-hand thread, I removed half the crests and turned it down to about ½in (12mm) diameter. I also turned down a small spigot at the end, ⁹⁄₃₂in (7mm) in diameter and ⅛in (3mm) deep. When the sides of this were removed by file or cutter, this constituted my excellent screwdriver.

Now for the moment of truth. Could I actually cut a left-hand inside screw on the cap? 'Some fool has done it and so can I,' quoth I, echoing young Bertram, 'and it won't take me a hundredweight of wood to find out.' I had three goes, actually. The result is sketched on page 57.

I had no bother striking the threads; I simply started from the back and pulled the chaser out – on the armrest of course. I found no more difficulty cutting a left- than I do a right-hand thread. A little trial and error and the cap fitted very well.

STEP FIVE

I screwed the cap on moderately hard, then ignored it while I struck a thread on the whole plug, to fit the breech, as sketched below.

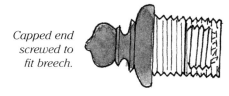

Capped end screwed to fit breech.

When I'd got a good fit I took off the cap, screwed it back lightly and tried it on the barrel again. It seemed a little tighter, so I ran the chaser along a couple more times. It fitted perfectly and the screw completely hid the join of the cap.

STEPS SIX, SEVEN AND EIGHT

There now remains just the muzzle plug to do. For step six, I cut the screw to fit nicely with an end to fit the countersink, and cut off 1/32in (1.5mm) proud.

Muzzle plug and slotting cutter.

For step seven, sketched above, replace the barrel in the chuck and turn the plug to a dome.

Finally, for step eight, use a hand-made slotting cutter to make a concave slot in the plug, 1/8in (3mm) wide. I did this by steadying my hands on the withdrawn tee rest, as I steered the plug carefully onto the cutter.

A good polish on the buff and we're done. The plug is in good and tight and the puzzle is to get it out and release the cannonball. What cannonball? You must make one of course, or find a steel ball that fits.

MODIFICATION

The customer most likely to enjoy these screw-guns was enthusiastic about them. He also knew something about similar puzzle guns and he requested a modification, which is sketched below. There is another join in the middle of the barrel and this screws on with a left-hand thread. This is the genuine place of concealment for the cannonball because the hole at the muzzle end is a blind one.

The cap upon the breech end screw-fits with an ordinary right-hand thread and the puzzler is supposed to find and penetrate the secret of the hidden screwdriver, open the muzzle plug and find it's been a red herring. They won't suspect that the middle of the gun unscrews in a fiendishly cunning anti-clockwise manner and will continue to puzzle about that rattling ball.

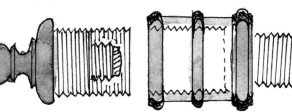 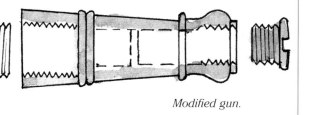

Modified gun.

If that's what he wants that's what he'll get. But my guess is that your average astute puzzler will go straight to the centre join and solve the problem – and never bother about silly screwdrivers. But it's all good clean fun – and I get paid for it too.

LITTLE FISH ARE SWEET

Quote from a letter from Bertram, 16 January, '50:

'. . . the reason firms can carry on a smooth and even flow of work is quite simple, but it doesn't apply in the case of a one-man business. If you go out asking for orders you will get them and, in many cases in such quantities that you just cannot cope with them.

'We cannot extend quickly enough to satisfy a customer who wants hundreds of pounds worth of work a week, therefore, altho' we often get a bite from a sizeable fish we dare not attempt to hook same.

'Since I have been here, I've been approached by a good many firms, but when I have to tell them I am on my own with no hope of extending, of course they have to go elsewhere.

'Consequently, we only get the scraps that other firms wouldn't look at. But these scraps keep coming in and being small and awkward you can get a fair price.'

Bertram had had his share of running a bigger show with half a dozen turners, not always turning out acceptable work, and he was far more contented on his own – and free to enjoy the odd day's fishing. One of his favourite saws was, 'little fish are sweet'.

IDENTICAL PIECES

One of my little fish is an antique dealer named Jane. I had a letter from her recently:

Dear Lovejoy,
Now here is a *real* challenge for you. Can you make me – identical in every respect as to colour, turning and carving – three of the

beautiful carved urn exactly as pattern [shown right]?
Lady Jane

They were finials, 1½in (38mm) high and ½in (12mm) in diameter. The panels of the shaped urn were seven in number and convex – more *difficile* (and handsome) than concave. I turned five – a straightforward job in the three-jaw.

Carved urn.

As the stipulation was 'identical in every respect' I had to try to make them 'near enough – that's egzackly!' Actually, this means that, being hand work they'll all be different. When I once apologized for this to the well-known treen collector Edward Pinto, for whom I did restorations, he assured me it was the small discrepancies that constitute the charm of hand-made work. But, I made them as nearly alike as I could, measuring every distance and diameter by dividers and callipers, and holding the pattern alongside the work to judge its verisimilitude and mark here and there with a pencil. It becomes quite a speedy process if you don't rush, always remembering that quality comes first, speed comes with practice.

THE TURNING BEGINS

The petalled spire, shown right, is done in four stages:

1 I mark nine divisions on the bottom rim, doing this by putting a pencil mark where the three chuck jaws come on the work, mark two points equidistantly between each third, then use a dental burr in an indispensable pin vice clamped in the three-jaw,

Petalled spire.

to make nine hollows between the lines.

2 With a conical burr in the three-jaw, I remove the corners of each hollow, leaving nine points.

3 With a fine vee cutter, I run lines from the inner vees of the points to the top flange. This gives nine petals.

4 Lastly, with a wider vee cutter, I make a scallop in the middle of each petal. My vee cutters are mainly made out of nails, shaping them in the three-jaw with a three square file as they revolve at speed.

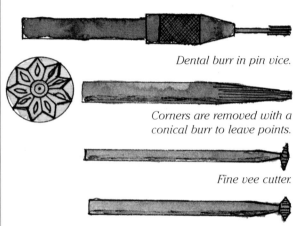

Dental burr in pin vice.

Corners are removed with a conical burr to leave points.

Fine vee cutter.

Wider vee cutter.

Saw teeth are then cut with a three square needle file. When making these cutters, or using them at speed, make sure you have no sleeves or neckties etc., to catch in the whirling jaws or the cutter, and don't use force, for obvious reasons.

We now come to the seven panels on the urn. These are pencilled on, but how do you divide? The top sketch, right, is drawn from below. The first line is due north, the second and third on either side of south. The east and west gaps are then divided into three, and if it looks evenly spaced to you, it'll be slightly better than

The seven panels are divided . . .

. . . and incised.

my pattern, which is by no means perfectly divided – and it doesn't matter a rap.

We start with our fine vee cutter running as fast as possible. Hold the spire in your left thumb and forefinger and the bottom in your right thumb and forefinger, and run it down the cutter from north to south.

I leave a gap of ³⁄₆₄in (1mm) below the bead before starting each line. The withdrawn tee rest gives support in steadying the hands. Make two very close lines on each of the seven pencil lines as shown bottom left.

The cutter will try to skid off the line until you teach it that *you* are in control, so 'relax-ezvous', hold the piece firmly, but without tension, and run it down gently so that if a skid occurs, it will only be a scratch.

Having made its first run down, you can then go over it confidently, as it has a track to follow. 'Never hurry now, for time's all sweet.' When the 14 lines are done, join the inside lines of each panel with a short horizontal line very close to the bead.

The convex panels are then scraped – or carved – to shape with a small inside tool, not only on either side of the perpendicular lines, but also next to the top horizontal line.

Small inside tool.

This is a real carving job, giving great satis-faction. I have a small, 3½in (90mm) vice secured to the end of the bed of my old Holtzapffel Eldorado by a single bolt, which allows me to move the vice in various positions at just the right height.

I have a big leg vice at the other end of the shop, but this little one is useful for jobs like this, or for fixing my oilstone firmly, thus avoiding the irritating habit of sending it flying off the bench onto the concrete floor when honing vigorously.

My boxwood clams, shown above right,

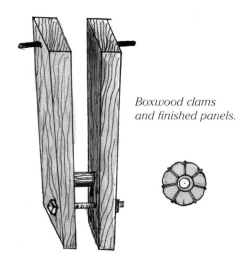

Boxwood clams and finished panels.

which have an adjusting bolt at the bottom and a short piece of rubber hose for a spring, are used with a rub of chalk to grip the work without bruising.

I grip the finial by its dowel on the far side of the vice and scrape the left side of each panel, very lightly at first, until it establishes the camber precisely alongside the line, without damaging it. When the seven are done, the clams are moved to the near side of the vice and the right side of the panels are done, giving a smooth, evenly rounded panel. The horizontal tops are then scraped to complete.

The bead immediately above is carved into a ring of pearls. This could be done on the ornamental lathe with a drill spindle in the slide rest – and beautiful it would look – but it wouldn't match the pattern, so I do it the hardwood and ivory turners' way by making a

little pearl cutter out of mild steel rod. Drill it accurately, about ³⁄₁₆in (5mm) deep and ³⁄₃₂in (2mm) in diameter.

Turn the end to a taper until it matches the diameter of the required bead. Then, with the cutter at high speed, and using the tee to support the hands, offer the bead up to the cutter by hand, eye and feel, and place each pearl correctly on the bead, without any gaps in between.

You may or may not find this easy, depending on the shape of the bead, the efficacy of the cutter, and your experience as a carver.

When you get to the last couple of pearls, space them by eye so that only careful observation could detect any discrepancy.

The finish is on the buff, with Cannings Crown or Lustre compo and afterwards the compo is brushed away with a toothbrush and hot, soapy water.

I made five so I could be sure of at least three good ones – the other two are only passables. The final word is from Lady Jane:

Dear Lovejoy,
You have really excelled yourself. My restorers are most impressed, especially by the finely detailed carved finials. Thank you so much for all your trouble.
Yours,
Jane (Alias Lady)

Carved finials and the tools used to make them.

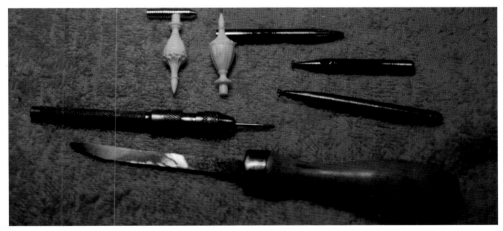

Chapter 10
Modern 'Luxuries' vs. Old-Fashioned TOOLS

Completed presentation chairman's hammer.

For nearly 40 years I have been writing about and encouraging the use of my DIY variable speed device, yet only one turner, the late Professor Debenham, the famous geologist of Scott's Antarctic expedition, actually adopted it.

I can now report two more who quite recently converted their lathes, and both are ecstatic in their praise, though not a whit surprised, for they could see clearly that the method couldn't fail.

One had just bought a very good Holtzapffel ornamental turning lathe formerly owned by my good old friend Wingco Cosby, Battle of Britain pilot, who died last year. The new owner visited me to make notes, in order to copy the set-up I have on my Holtz Eldorado lathe.

The beauty of it is that not only is the method effective for the headstock, but, with the addition of two more pulleys (one of them a sprung jockey), the overhead gear is also foot-

63

Left An old ivory gavel, turned by Bertram in the thirties.

controlled variable speed. This greatly improves the cutting as well as reducing the wear on the cutting frames, and enhances the pleasure of working 100% – something not to be sneezed at when the main purpose of our lathe work is the pursuit of pleasure. If you actually get paid you should regard it as a bonus.

In my opinion, this variable speed set-up is handsome and will appeal to those who enjoy seeing belts, pulleys and such like accoutrements of character. It's also quite safe because it can be stopped instantly in any circumstance.

> # THE main purpose of our lathe work is the pursuit of pleasure – if you actually get paid you should regard it as a bonus

Today, machinery is under cover and hidden from view, and if anyone gives the slightest indication that he or she is enjoying something or finding it interesting, this is severely frowned upon by indigenous or EEC bureaucrats, most of whom are abysmally ignorant of any type of craft and obdurately impervious to the blandishments of craftspeople.

PROPAGANDA

Surprisingly, they are occasionally supported by actual work people, who have been subjected to propaganda so insidiously over the past half century that they're uncomfortable if any machine shop doesn't look – and feel – as clinical as a public privy.

A workshop that looks like a real turning shop, or a forge, or a mill, as some of us used to know 'em, has got to be transported lock, stock and cobweb to one o' them outdoor museums.

I visited one near Cardiff a few years ago. It

had a street of ancient terrace houses and damned if we didn't spot the very kitchen with hearth and range we started our married life in – and very nice it was.

There was a turning shop there, complete with resident turner/carver with such a fine reputation that no less than 10 of his fans contacted me to recommend him. Sadly, he was too busy to be disturbed when we were there.

I said to Olive, 'I'd like to bring my Jonathan Muckle lathe here, open the doors and wake 'em up with a chess set.' I'll wager some factory inspector has run his rule over the joint and precluded every damn thing that could possibly promote interest.

DANGEROUS TOOLS

They have ladies going round now trying to stop turners sanding their work. And as such dangerous tools as skew chisels are *verboten*, by thunder, it needs sanding. There will be a very red-faced factory inspector limping away from *my* shop if they try stopping old Bill, I promise you.

CONVERSION

The chap who converted his Holtz was so delighted with the excellence of its new found ability that he invited comment from the distaff side of the family – his wife and ma-in-law.

'Oh dear!' they said, 'you *have* made a mess of it!' He tried to explain but, bless you, it's always a mistake. Uncle Zebedee told me, 'Never explain – your friends don't need it and your enemies won't believe it.'

My other friend who was so pleased with his converted plain lathe told the good news to the great ornamental turner-in-chief, – no names, no PD – and *he* said, 'Ooh! you've mucked up your lathe.'

Yet another ornamental turning wizard tutted sympathetically when he heard about it. 'You should've bought an electrical variable speed.' It was a really efficacious, electronic

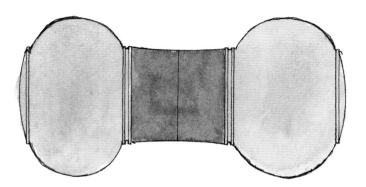

The original drawing from which the dimensions were set.

masterpiece, and only 500-odd quid. And if it goes 'on the blink', the engineer will undoubtedly fix it if you can hang on a fortnight and fork out half the purchase price.

However, altho' we old-fashioned turners are spared these modern luxuries, I have to say that variable-speed devices are rapidly improving all the time and I'd hate to be accused of Luddist tendencies!

GAVEL

My friend Walther had a little job for me a while back, which was quite attractive, though elementary. It was simply a presentation chairman's hammer, or gavel, with a concealed compartment containing a pen which, it was envisaged, could be slipped into the hollow handle from the head end.

This would weaken the handle at its slender part, so I suggested decorative beads at the meaty part, disguising the screw join. They hadn't thought of that would you believe?

African blackwood would be used for the handle and middle section of the head, while the ends would be old billiard balls. For those who have asked what they can make out of these ancient spheres, this is one suggestion.

I remember when merchants had barrels of them at a shilling each. But that was when a bob was worth a fiver of today's so-called money. I used them to make rattles, which required a diameter of 1½in (38mm), and out of a dozen old balls, four would be too cracked to use. In the restoration trade, old cracked stuff is often a *sine qua non*, so nothing is thrown away.

FREE FROM CRACKS

Today, these balls often cost £2–8 each, but I draw the line at a fiver – unless they are uncommonly free from cracks.

It's essential to make a drawing, something like my sketch shown above, however rough, in order to arrive at the dimensions you want. Unless you determine the exact dimensions and design in advance you will spoil your material, and this is a bad habit which no good worker can tolerate.

This was to be a large hammer, with a handle at least 10in (255mm) long. Billiard balls are usually of 2⅛in (55mm) in diameter, so I selected a couple with the least cracks, which were fairly evenly coloured.

Should they be noticeably at variance in colour, they can be immersed in hydrogen peroxide for a day or so, in the light. I use 25 volume hydrogen peroxide to 1–4 parts water. However, as the ends are to be separated by blackwood, a slight difference will pass unnoticed.

Normally I clamp them – forcibly – in the three- or four-jaw, but I couldn't afford the bruises, as the diameter had to be maximum and a bruise could waste ⅟₁₆ or ⅛in (2 or 3mm), so I tapped them into a wood cup chuck, and

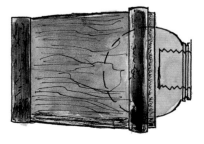

The balls were tapped into a wooden cup chuck.

turned them in my 8in (203mm) 'basher'.

This is a heavy great headstock at the end of my 12ft (3.6m) timber bench and it is driven by a ⅓HP sewing machine clutch motor connected to a foot pedal, so again, I have perfect variable speed.

Apart from cleaning (or excavating) the motor and replacing the clutch leather (myself), that motor – and an identical one that drives my Muckle – have run without trouble for 40 years.

The old lathe rattles a bit, but comes in handy for many jobs; sawing, grinding and polishing mainly. I don't know how old it is, but Bertram always had it, and I had new bearings made in 1962.

VARIOUS SIZES

There are many cup chucks, in various woods and sizes, which cover my normal needs. All the hardwood and ivory turners kept dozens of these wooden chucks and iron cup chucks, which they stopped with boxwood and other materials. They used self-centring chucks very little by comparison – and *never* wasted money on new ones.

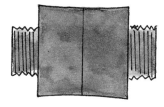
Mid-section of gavel head.

Cutting the screw on the centre piece.

The ball turned to shape.

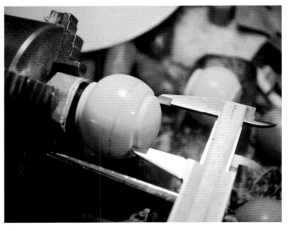
Ensuring accuracy while turning the heads.

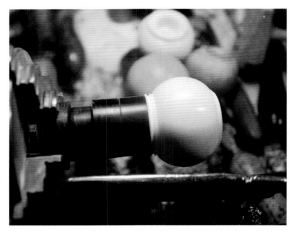
One head beautifully completed.

First turning, face off the front and turn a decorative hollow delicately, with a ¹⁄₁₆in (1.5mm) (or thereabouts) round tool. Bore and open a hole, about ¾in (20mm) in diameter and ¾in (20mm) deep, and cut an inside thread about 16 teeth per inch. If you find you're getting a 32 thread, double the speed of the traverse of the chaser, because you're cutting a double-start thread.

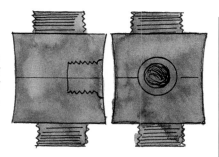

Mid-section of gavel head threaded and countersunk.

Knock out the ball and repeat on the second one, getting the diameter of the decorative hollow exactly the same and the thread very similar. The African blackwood mid-section of the head, shown on page 66, is quite straightforward, and turned in the four-jaw.

Having cut a thread to fit one ball, it may be finished *in situ*, following the details of your drawing and tapping it to run perfectly true if necessary. Always do the crackiest ball first, because the second has to match exactly and you never know how defective a ball is.

I made a slight hollow curve in the black section and turned a centre line with a flat point tool. When reversing the section to deal with the other end, I lapped some abrasive paper around it for protection, and finished the second ball to the identical dimensions, again tapping it dead true.

It's important to get the two male screw lengths exactly alike because, when gripped 'thwartships' in a chuck to turn the inside screw for the handle, the centre line you've made with the point tool must be dead centre in the chuck.

Often, I tap it in a large cup chuck sideways, assisting the grip on the ends with several folds of abrasive paper, but today I gripped it in a Holtz two-jaw which was sitting there doing nothing. I still protected the ends, but this time I cut two slender oblongs of blackwood accurately on a delightful Burgess-type band saw, knocked down to me for £55 at the last auction of the Society of Ornamental Turners' AGM. It stands conveniently on the same bench as my 8in (203mm) 'basher'.

MANY 'improvements' have a weak point that prevents them being quite indispensable, altho', on rare occasions they're useful

Don't use much pressure on the tools in boring out and cutting the 16 thread for the handle, in case it comes out of the chuck, because you don't want the trouble of trying to replace it.

I made the hole a bit too large – about $^{23}/_{32}$in (18mm) in diameter, when $^{5}/_{8}$in (15mm) would have done, but 'twill serve. Make a nice hollow countersink for the end bead of the handle to bed down upon, as shown below.

Centre piece hollowed, threaded with 16 chaser and countersunk.

Main handle turned to shape.

*Spear drill used to drill
the hole in the handle to take the pen.*

Next, the handle. I had cut an 8in (203mm) length of square stock, and fixed it between the four-jaw and the new live centre to turn one end down, before reversing it to grip the round end firmly. The skew picks up the grain on blackwood, which is almost as hard as ivory, so I prefer the finish from my square tool.

Also, while live centres are convenient for many jobs, the extra bearing vibrates and makes the actual turning less pleasant than when using the dead centre. So many 'improvements' have a weak point that prevents them being quite indispensable, altho', on rare occasions they're useful.

I turned a spigot for a male thread before taking it out and replacing it with the top 3in (75mm) of the handle. When turned, I made four beads with the point tool, next to the join.

I then moved about 3ft (1m) to the right, along the bench, to my 1½in (38mm) hollow mandrel, fixed the handle in the three-jaw and cut the thread to fit the head, making the first bead bed nicely down.

Reversing the handle, I cut another male thread to screw into the top part. I then drilled a hole to receive the slender metal pen. I am well equipped with spear drills up to ⅝in (15mm) for this type of job. Some I have made myself, but other, rather

better ones are stamped 'H & D' which stands for Holtzapffel and Deyerlein – and the latter left the partnership about 1820.

The top of the pen projected about 2in (50mm), so when I clamped the top in the three-jaw and cut an inside thread which fitted the main handle perfectly, I drilled the top to accommodate the whole pen. Accuracy of drilling is, of course, far easier when you use the armrest.

After papering well and truly, and waxing with 0000 steel wool, I gave it a good buff polish and pronounced the job 'pretty good old son'. I then took the whole thing apart in six pieces, including the pen, and packed them as carefully as though they were eggs. Old Walther couldn't have been more pleased!

*The hammer in six separate pieces,
showing the concealed pen.*

Chapter 11
Monotony or PLEASURE

*B*oxing Day '94. There's even more pleasure than usual in my snug little turning shop, as I can enjoy a few hours away from the world's Saturnalian revels.

I've set a very low work target for today, just a couple of old ivory finials and a few hundred words in the cheap, lined notebook I use for rough drafts when 'penning my stunners'.

Olive has some ironing to catch up on and anything we particularly fancy on TV is safely booked into the video to enjoy – or sleep through – at leisure.

Leisure, when you have earned it by honest toil, is far more pleasurable than when it's over-indulged in for whole days in weary succession.

Above *Just turning.*

Many a man would envy me I know, so I was recently surprised to read woodturning described as ' . . . a mindless occupation . . . the epitome of monotony.' Well! they can't touch you for doing it or writing about it, I'm glad to say. I can best reply in the words of the poet:

> But don't you stop in the turner's shop
>   with a mind 'whence all has fled,
> You must clear the way for the turner's
>   spray or the slap from an overhead.
> You may crack your shin on a spare-gear
>   tin or your elbow against a rest,
> But if you step in with a mind less dim on
>   an honest, genuine quest,
> It's a welcome true and a 'how do ye do'
>   and a yarn with one o' the best.

Not everyone has to like turnery – of course they don't. But you may well ask, what mind-boggling occupation stimulates the working hours of our critic? Actually he's a stick whittler. Eh? Pardon?

He whittles sticks. So, what's wrong with that? Absolutely nothing. I like his work. But even if I felt it lacked a modicum of vital interest, I'd have more tact and kindness than to say so.

It's an unhappy person who criticizes another's trade, and smacks of sour grapes. I can think of many jobs that would bore me rigid, but someone likes them, and so could I if they came my way. If I were younger I could probably enjoy stacking planks.

To me, the epitome of monotony is the chap who does nothing and then complains that life is so boring he has to get into mischief. Let us therefore be encouraging to fellow workers – there aren't so many of us left.

FINIALS

But I came into the shop with the intention of setting the lathe going, so from a box of enders I sorted a couple that would yield the finials,

and I hubbed them to go in the three-jaw chuck.

I fixed one in the chuck very firmly by the top end and turned down the other end with a ⅜in (10mm) spindle gouge, smoothing it to a diameter slightly bigger than the bottom flange next to the spigot.

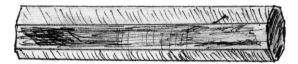

A piece from the box of enders.

The second piece was done in the same way, which is always the way when more than one is called for. The finials could now be turned in one go, gripping the small end in the three- or four-jaw chuck.

Using a good vernier calliper to test each measurement as it came, I achieved a near perfect likeness, by regularly holding the pattern against the turning to compare. The trained eye spots the smallest disparity, but without trained hands would be powerless.

All who attempt such work must, by persistence, stick with it – and be sure to enjoy it – until the ability comes. Perfection is what we're aiming for, but not really hoping to actually reach, if we're wise, for if it could be attained we'd have reached our goal with nothing left to strive for.

I've had a lifetime of turning, yet know of many who can – and do – teach me a lot. Hopefully, there will always be some whose work is presently beyond my reach.

Top part of the finial.

I turned the top part with a small round tool (cleanly honed) on the armrest, which helps greatly in getting a precise, flowing shape. Indeed, if the shape is slightly impaired, I may leave out both armrest and tool rest, and apply the round tool in a trailing, side-to-side, butterfly's-wing cut, free hand. This clears away any bumps or lines that impair the perfect curve.

The lower half I did with the same small round tool and a ¼in (6mm) flat tool. Three grades of abrasive paper ensured a perfect finish. I turned down the spigot and reversed the finial.

The finial shape.

There's a nick about ⁹⁄₃₂in (7mm) inside the jaws, within which will fit the tiny bead, but the jaws in the four-jaw have a narrower and sharper gripping surface than those in the three-jaw, so it was the latter I used, to avoid bruising.

I tightened it with discreet pressure which caused little harm, remembering that this was antique restoration so sparkling newness was hardly necessary. To be sure, I could not apply much pressure to the tool or I would have needed to tighten too much – so I turned down the spigot gingerly, with ⅛in (3mm) round and small flat tools.

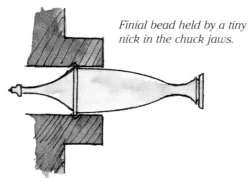

Finial bead held by a tiny nick in the chuck jaws.

The second finial was slightly longer, sufficient to grip in the chuck without having to reverse, but there was almost no room to cut it off with a normal screever, so I used my abnormal one, made from the inevitable triangular file. This has an extremely short blade, only 0.5mm thin. It comes in quite handy in my trade.

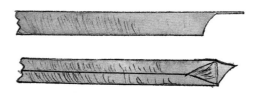

Screever with 0.5mm thick blade made from triangular file.

I can buff polish unaided, but find it expedient – and therefore recommend it to you – to grip the spigot in a small, No. 1, morse taper drill chuck, to obviate the danger of the buff sending it flying to the most inaccessible nether regions below the benches, where it may never be seen again.

To get the finials the same colour as the pattern, I steeped them in half a cupful of hot, but not too strong, tea (no milk or sugar, please), with a dash of ascetic acid vinegar as a mordant.

I needed a small piece of polished ivory as a test piece and found an ancient, 1in (25mm) cigarette tube in an old Balkan Sobranie tobacco tin. I'd smoked the tobacco overseas in the RAF 50 years back, but the redolence was as fresh and delightful as when new – and I quit smoking 30 years ago.

If you use a test piece, of course, the colour usually goes exactly as you want it, as it did in this case. But if you chance it and put work straight in, you may depend it will be wrong. A polish on the swansdown mop, and that's it.

CHUCKS

Back to the subject of three- and four-jaw chucks. I hadn't a four-jaw until about three years ago, when I gave a 3in (75mm), geared scroll, three-jaw to a friend who wanted it urgently. 'A friend in need is a so-and-so nuisance', 'tis said, but I often find an ultimate benefit from my sacrifice – as in this curious case.

I contacted a firm noted for good English chucks and was horrified to learn I couldn't replace the 3in (75mm), geared scroll, three-jaw and that a lever scroll one – which is not so good – would cost over £200.

I had to have one, so took delivery of it. At the next meeting of the Society of Ornamental Turners I asked a couple of the chaps about chucks and prices and was advised to buy Czech chucks from a particular firm, as they were a fraction of the price of the English, and were known by long experience to be excellent and reliable.

I sent for their catalogue, was absolutely amazed and, as a result, ordered three geared scroll chucks – one 3in (76mm) and one 4in (102mm) three-jaw, and a 4in (102mm) four-jaw. The total cost was a little over £100. They've been the best chucks I've ever had.

SECURING RETURNS

The new lever scroll chuck was now surplus to my requirements and still in its box, brand new and unused. I therefore contacted the supplier and asked if they'd be kind enough to take it back. They readily agreed and I returned the chuck at once. More than a year later, after numerous phone calls and letters, the money had still not been returned. I had given it up as a bad job when I heard of an experience which may be of help to anyone who meets with a similar problem.

Measuring tool rack, also for repetition work.

A city gent found himself due for a refund from British Rail, but could get nothing done about it. The buck was passed to and fro but no-one bothered to do anything.

On the advice of some old genius he addressed his claim to the absolute head of BR, and within a week had a letter from the chief expressing his 'horror' and making complete restitution.

I wrote forthwith to 'The Managing Director in Person' of my dilatory firm and sent it special delivery, marked 'Private and Personal'. Again, I had complete satisfaction in a few days. To anyone in the same fix I therefore advise, 'Go thou and do likewise'.

Bench tool rack for repetition work.

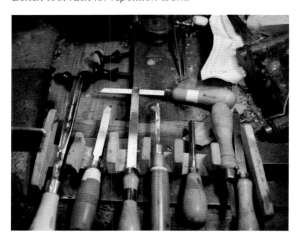

ORGAN DRAW-STOP KNOBS

The last job I got 'under the wire' before the Christmas break was 27 organ drawstop knobs in African blackwood (supplied), with white casein inserts. It's the type of work I do more than any other, but I don't tire of it because of the precision needed to get them all alike. When

Finished organ drawstop knob, not recessed in this case.

Bert Marsh tires of turning bowls, then I might consider chucking drawstop knobs.

If I get a serious tool slip it's not yet another 'design opportunity' as in some 'one off' jobs – it's scrap! The fact that I didn't have to scrap one was unusual, explained by the soundness of the wood – and long experience. I don't always get away with it with rosewood, but African blackwood, like ivory, is a scraping tool material.

I roughed down with a gouge, but the shaping called for a round tool. Much as I enjoy using a gouge to get a clean shape in rosewood, the gouge picked up the grain in this exceptionally hard blackwood.

As I've often said, 'scraping' tools do *not* scrape hard materials. It's the way you use a tool, and the type of material, that makes a scraper – a word which applies more to turners than tools. (If I harp on certain points a great deal, mark it down under 'Repetition for Emphasis'.)

The wood had been supplied in square, 4in (100mm) lengths, so I began by fixing these lengths in the four-jaw, and turning their ends to fit a brass cup chuck on my Holtz Vampire lathe. This was made by Holtzapffel and Deyerlein in 1813 for £136, so you can count it a good 'un.

I was working to a thou here – without a mike – to get the wood to enter the chuck just ⅛in (3mm), but I didn't measure it – two or three trials and it was there.

I use a slightly smaller chuck if necessary, because the art of the turner is to accumulate all the tools and accoutrements that you need and never throw anything away. Here's what Ashley Iles said about a marvellous Sheffield craftsman:

'In 30 years nothing, absolutely nothing, has been thrown away. It was all over the floor, leaving only a zig-zag path through, but mostly over it.

'It went up all the walls to the ceiling. Only a man in complete command of his craft could get away with such eccentricity'. I haven't quite got that far – but give me time.

The blank was driven – not bashed and shattered – into the chuck with a 1½lb. (680g), short-handled, ball pein hammer. Don't expect it to hold if you don't chalk the wood first. And if your lathe falls apart, I should go out and get a good one. All good lathes can stand a bashing, but remember, we are not really bashing, but driving the work into the chuck.

Makers, to be on the safe side, tell you this should be done on the bench, but I've never seen anyone do this successfully, because you can't check truth unless the chuck is on the mandrel. In any case, good makers also tell you *not* to use the lathe bench as an anvil. I never do. Well . . . hardly ever.

For repetition work I keep my measuring tools hanging on a rack and my turning tools on a bench rack, all in chronological order.

After roughing down to size with a gouge (I shan't specify which, but old timers will probably give a knowing grin when I say 'the gouge that cuts'), I faced the surface with my triangular point tool.

I then made a shallow recess with a ⅛in (3mm), long-handled round tool, and opened it out to a precise diameter with perfect, clean, straight sides with my same sharp point tool – all on the armrest. I could have used a side tool, but the point tool is sharper, keeps its edge longer and can be touched on the grindstone in half a minute.

The rest was simply a careful, unhurried piece of turning. If you try to make these knobs, make sure you avoid dig-ins because, if

Skimming down casein blanks to fit each knob individually. A wood plug of slightly less diameter facilitates the quick centring of each blank in the four-jaw chuck.

Each knob has a glued inset. A two-piece boxwood collet enables the knob to be secured in the four-jaw chuck for facing off with round tool and square tool, on the armrest.

the work jerks out of the chuck it is more difficult to return it accurately, and a small piece of wood has to be used within the recess to avoid damage.

Every diameter and distance has to be measured, so the first knob will take a lot longer to turn than the tenth, no matter how long you've been turning.

Before I turned down the end to make the dowel, I finished with three grades of abrasive, 0000 steel wool and wax. The photo, top, shows the casein blanks being turned down to fit each knob individually.

A wood plug of slightly less diameter helps

to chuck the blank accurately and quickly. After gluing them in with Araldite, a two-piece boxwood collet enables you to secure the knob in the four-jaw for facing off the insert to a gentle dome, as shown in the photo below left, with round and square tools on the armrest.

My finished batch of work, 'sparkling with pleasure' after a polish on the calico buff with Cannings Lustre compo, is shown below.

The finished batch of organ drawstop knobs.

MONOTONY

My thoughts keep returning to the almost incredible words, '. . . a mindless occupation . . . the epitome of monotony!' How could this be? I ask myself. And half an answer eventually presents itself. Supposing I had no customers and no outlet for my work. Supposing I had to begin marketing from scratch. Without custom, turning items you can't sell could indeed be the epitome of monotony, unless you are turning purely for pleasure.

I have no glib answer here, but what I'd do is what I did 40 years ago. I contacted lots of possible firms that might be interested in my work, submitting samples and often accepting some 'workhouse' jobs to keep the pot boiling.

If you can survive for a couple of years, reliable customers *will* materialize. There are two provisos. Your work *must* be undeniably good, and your service reliable for, as the book of Proverbs says, 'A good name is better than abundant riches'.

Chapter 12
Dragonfly BROOCH

Above *Carving Vandykes.*

T his dragonfly is a perfect project for beginners as it cannot fail to turn out well – unless one is absolutely determined. Suitable material is up to you. Mine used to be thin ivory waste, but bone, plastic or any handsome hardwood, will do.

CUTTING OUT

First draw the shape on a piece of card. I cut up tea cartons for this purpose. Two are required; the wings with head and thorax, and the curved body.

A finished brooch.

75

Cut them out with scissors, place them on top of your ¼in (6mm) thick material, and pencil carefully around them. Cut them out on the band saw – I used my 6in (152) circular saw.

I don't make them in one piece because they are liable to snap during the vice work. The body is made with six rounded cones and the top is invisibly joined to the thorax with a thin dowel, after finishing.

To start, I use my hub, the main cutter I use for roughing out, and sometimes more precise work. When using this tool, I've noticed looks of apprehension on some faces in the audience, some who clearly regard it as dangerous. The teeth – about 14 teeth per inch – aren't very sharp and are quite safe. There are cutters I'd never use. One, described by Ashley Iles in his lovely book *Memories of a Sheffield Tool Maker*, is a razor-sharp steel one, 14in (350mm) in diameter and 3in (75mm) thick.

The hub – the main cutter I use for roughing out.

It runs backwards and the operator works on the top, free hand. It's about as safe as a guardless spindle moulder. The dear little cutters I use wouldn't hurt a fly.

In the first cutting of the wings I make the top flat and remove the bark, holding and moving the piece low down on the cutter, about 7 o'clock, and using no force.

In this way it's unlikely to snatch, but if it does, your fingers are holding the piece at the sides and will not be whipped into the cutter. If the last four words make you nervous, there's no need. We are using a mild steel cutter with small teeth that are not razor sharp.

All fear will vanish when you take a stick of wood long enough to give plenty of room to keep your fingers clear, and just shape the wood and see how that cutter behaves. Five minutes should convince you the hazards are minimal – the worst nick you'll ever get will be cured by a lick and a strip o' plaster. Some turners seem to wear a perpetual plaster on one or other of their fingers – and they don't use cutters.

There is far more danger from a three or four-jaw chuck if you are using one that hasn't had the sharp edges ground off.

I use a much bigger cutter with about 6 teeth per inch when I have heavier work to do and no time to waste tickling the stuff on baby cutters. And I assure you I'm in no danger.

SHAPING THE UNDERSIDE

We have flattened the top nicely, re-pencilled the shape with our template, and now we embark on the underside, bringing it to a uniform thickness – not exceeding ¼in (6mm) – and rounding it so the underside meets the top at an angle of 45°.

A selection of my cutters.

Much more can be achieved with the hub than you would think, and in spindle carving, always do as much as possible with each cutter as you progress with the job. This is even more important when making a number of the same items. They are far more likely to be alike, and your skill and speed improves with each one although, of course, quality must never be sacrificed for speed, unless – as often used to be the case – the customer knocks you down to so low a price that he can't expect top quality.

> # YOU MUST remember that all tools are to be used to the best advantage of the finished job and not because someone advocates them

As you look at the shape and the material to be removed outside the pencil line, you either see that the hub can get at it safely or not – that includes rounding the head. But go only as far as your limitations and experience allow, rather than take one too many risks and make a horrid gash in the outline, which must be perfect and unblemished if you don't want to chuck it in the 'waster box'.

That's an old Bertram expression. He worked for a firm in Walsall in his young days at the turn o' the century, and, having turned his first batch of work, the guv'nor – to put him down a trifle – said, 'They're not *too* bad – of course, they'll have to go in the waster box.'

At this point my daughter Ginette, to whom I was reading this, said, 'One of these days you'll be introduced as 'the turn o' the century!' Flattery gets her everywhere.

The next cutter I use is the narrow vee. With this tool, important little places around the head and thorax and the underwing vees can be

Narrow vee cutter.

dealt with, not with finesse, but, to save time, with the files, rasps, rifflers and scrapers with which the finish is achieved in the vice.

You must remember that all tools are to be used to the best advantage of the finished job and not because someone advocates them. Therefore, as soon as one tool becomes a liability and you can't be certain its continued use will not bring disaster, drop it and use something safer. Experience is the best teacher.

HEAD AND THORAX

There is another little cutter I use to trim between the head and wings. It's an easily made little slotting cutter, as sketched below.

Slotting cutter for trimming between head and wings.

Small, flat cutter for shaping the wings.

The middle line that divides the upper and lower pairs of wings is pencilled firmly in and a small flat cutter, sketched left, is run along it from the lower wing side so that these wings are slightly below the level of the uppers.

There is an X in the middle of the thorax, and not only is its centre the beginning of the outline of all four wings, but the middle

Mid-line on the wings made with the cutter.

Two small 'x' cutters made from 4in (102mm) nails.

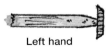
Left hand

Right hand

dividing line I've just described passes right through it. I carve this X with two small cutters, made in 10 minutes from a couple of 4in (102mm) nails.

Now, take careful note. With the left-hand cutter you cut in the upper left and lower right arms of the X, and with the right-hand cutter, the upper right and lower left arms of the X. You must work from the line of the wing to the centre of the X – and not beyond the centre. Thus, you will have an uninterrupted outline of each wing, right to the centre of the thorax.

The neck and thorax have to be nicely rounded and so do the underwings at all parts. To help me here, I use a small conical cutter, moving the work in all directions to bring the cutter to bear on each part, where it can achieve the shape I'm after. Although completely free hand, I have the tee rest a few inches back, to support the hands where necessary.

Small conical cutter for shaping.

Moving the work against the cutter might appear an unsatisfactory method of carving, because the work is never the same way up for more than a few seconds.

Once, long ago, I procured a flexible drive because I'd always had an idea that if I could fix the work in the vice like a *real* carver, I could work upon it with my cutters in the flexible drive much more controllably.

FLEXIBLE DRIVE

I can tell you straight away that it was 'double useless' (as my old RAF mate Morgan used to say

so scathingly), because the cutters skidded off in all directions, and although suitable for boring or working in tiny areas, as in dentistry, it didn't work for shaping.

After that experience I found that to have the cutters revolving at high speed in the lathe worked 10 times better because they were 'fixed and immutable like the laws of the Swedes and the Nasturtiums', as Coker of the fifth used to say.

You could put on the pressure to speed the carving with ease and facility. When you grow accustomed to bringing the workpiece to the cutter the work is examined right way up, quickly brought to the cutter, and moved to carve the portion needing attention, then examined right way up again. The work is on the move all the time and the hand and eye are such good pals it's as though one's very fingers have eyes.

FINISHING

When the cutters have 'gone about as far as they can go,' then it's to the vice with its hardwood clams, well chalked so the work won't slip. I then file, scrape and smooth with glass cloth (or other suitable abrasive). I have a variety of small (and larger) files, floats, rasps and rifflers, and I scrape with a small inside turning tool until the whole is shaped and smoothed to perfection.

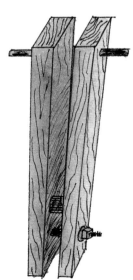

The rounded head and thorax are papered to shape with thin strips of glass cloth, and the inside tool scrapes the dividing line on the wings and the X so that, when polished on the buff – what else – no roughness is noticeable.

Hardwood vice clams, sprung with a piece of rubber hose.

Rear view of the dragonfly.

A view from the rear end looks as sketched above. The wings taper down, but there is a flat part in the middle to accommodate the narrow pin which may be Araldited, but which I choose to drill and tap for two 8BA brass screws.

The wing tops are smooth and flat, but now I make 18 shallow oval depressions in them, exactly as marked below. These are achieved first with a spherical cutter, then I black them all with pencil and – in the clams – scrape them smooth with a round nose tool.

Two grooves go right over the top of the head, made with a rounded cutter – or you may use a rat-tailed file, lapping it with fine abrasive paper to finish. The whole is then polished.

BODY

Now for the body. Marked out with the aid of a card template, it is cut out on the band saw and cuttered into six rounded cones, as in the sketch below, a bit on the oval side in section and not too precise if we want some

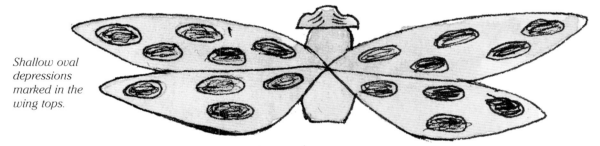

Shallow oval depressions marked in the wing tops.

They should polish quite well, but, because it is the finishing touches that typify the work – not so much the skilled operator, but the thorough one – I fix a little felt bob in the three-jaw, and bring to mirror finish each of those 18 hollows.

Spherical cutter or burr for marking the hollows.

Felt bobs of a variety of shapes may be obtained and screwed onto the same screw as the buff. Cannings Lustre is the polishing compo. The danger of using felt bobs is that too much pressure burns and makes unacceptable marks, so polish 'judiciously'.

Rounded cutter for grooving the head.

character in our work.

The tail ends in a vee and the top is flattened. It's about ³⁄₁₆in (5mm) in diameter. The finishing vice work is done with strips of glass cloth and the body is polished on the buff.

Six rounded cones for the body.

With a small, flat file, both joining surfaces (the bottom of the thorax and top of the body) are matched up so that the diameters and shape are compatible. Unless this is perfect, the join will be noticeable.

The ends are centre marked and a hole, about ³⁄₃₂in (2.5mm) in diameter and ³⁄₁₆in (5mm) deep, drilled. A bone or ivory dowel is turned to fit and Araldite will secure it so no-one would know it isn't a one-piece brooch.

All the cutters I use are those that come to hand, because I never make a special one if I have something that is near enough, so the sketches are merely to give a rough idea.

I don't think I can add anything more to these detailed instructions. I used to make the brooches for £12 each, but it gradually went up to £20 at the end. And very nice they were. 'Mr Jones,' they said, 'we *love* getting your parcels.' Happy days! I wish I were making a dozen now.

ORNAMENTAL VERSATILITY

I consider anything made on the lathe to be suitable material for my column. I leave as little as possible to be done off the lathe – and sometimes it's very little indeed.

When I discovered ornamental turning in 1948, and learnt that the ornamental turning lathe was a universal turning, shaping, milling and carving machine, I was tremendously interested. I soon found, however, that for trade work, time alone would preclude its use.

THE HAND and eye are such good pals it's as though one's very fingers have eyes

My spindle carving methods on the plain lathe were sufficient to cover most of my work, and my use of the ornamental turning lathe was limited to high days and luxuries. Today, the things I can't do without the ornamental turning lathe turn up rarely, but when they do they highlight its amazing value and versatility.

Forty years ago, the Society of Ornamental Turners roped me in to give a talk on making Staunton chessmen. As I was explaining how I made crude carving cutters out of nails and bolts etc., Captain Davis, an old sea dog with a black eye patch, who was one of our top ornamental turners, was so startled he piped up, 'My God Jones, you don't need a lathe at all'.

However, there is no comparison or rivalry between hand work and ornamental turning – each has its own particular charm, and I usually blend the two, which go together anyway.

Bertram had no time for ornamental turning, as it was foreign to his nature, but when a client of his offered him a Holtzapffel, 5in (127mm), screw mandrel ornamental turning outfit, he bought it for me.

It wasn't cheap – 40 quid was a lot in the fifties. A month later he came down from his little shop in the Cotswolds to London to see me. His first words were, 'Let's see this Eldorado of yours.' And that's why I called it the Eldorado from then on.

I never tired of watching him carving with his many cutters in the lathe, which he always enjoyed. His father, Lewis Jones (1850–1914), was a first class spindle carver – as well as turner – shining particularly at bone and ivory parasol handles with motifs of mice running up foliage etc.

Stop Press. I did another demo day in February, but the morning session was a disaster. So please note – if you want to be assured you are *not* the only turner who makes a dog's breakfast of the whole rigmarole, book BJ, one of the older, better, cheaper acts. It's an educational experience. When you leave, you'll say, 'That's taught *me* something.'

Chapter 13
Words of ADVICE

Above *Screw cutting*.

Whated writing about turning, it's never safe to assume that every reader understands you. I see this when, now and then, I meet readers who reveal my shortcomings.

Personally, I find it hard to follow written instructions, even when the writer has clearly covered every step he feels is important. If there's any ambiguity, the chain is broken and I may give up.

I used to blame it on my thickheadedness, until I read what Marcel Proust wrote about highly intelligent people who lack the ability to make their precise meaning crystal clear. That cheered me up no end.

There must be many who would agree with the reader who wrote, 'I'm trying to pick up knowledge from reading, but there's nothing to beat constant practice'.

The person who practises unremittingly will probably win through in the end, but the idea behind shared experience is to enable readers to avoid pitfalls, thus improving their practice.

It's only when we read the methods and experiences of others, or watch them at demos or on video, that we realize how very different we all are.

Although I've been turning for a long time,

I've led a sheltered, solitary life, and my methods, concentrated mainly on ivory and other hard materials, place me in the beginners' situation so far as pukka woodturning is concerned.

I avidly study the best in the hope that I might become proficient in all branches of turnery. I'm tempted to try unfamilar things at demos sometimes, but discretion triumphs as a rule. I'd most likely come a bigger cropper than I normally do.

SHARPENING CHASERS

Screw cutting by hand chaser is catching on, and friends are showing me samples of their successes and failures. How to sharpen the chaser is a question I've been asked a few times.

For the outside chaser, the top surface is hollow ground on top of the grinding wheel. This is easy on mine, which I use on a boxwood chuck which screws onto my 8in (200mm) 'basher' lathe, and runs at about 2,200rpm.

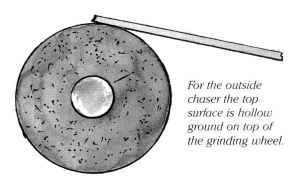

For the outside chaser the top surface is hollow ground on top of the grinding wheel.

On a bench grinder I can't even see the top of the wheel, so I crouch uncomfortably and hope for the best. But take no notice of me – it's what you get used to.

I paid 30 quid for a 6 teeth per inch inside chaser, so I don't gaily grind things away, as seems to be the fashion with wealthier turners. Touch it lightly on the wheel, just enough to ensure each tooth is sharp.

If the first, or leading, tooth is dull it won't cut, so watch that. Subsequently re-sharpen by rubbing it face down on a medium India oilstone, or similar. Grind only when that doesn't work so well.

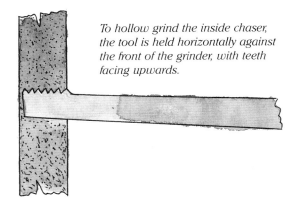

To hollow grind the inside chaser, the tool is held horizontally against the front of the grinder, with teeth facing upwards.

To hollow grind the inside chaser, the tool is held horizontally against the front of the grinder, with teeth facing upwards. The parts where the tool rubs the tee rest (or armrest for the inside chaser) should be smoothed on the oilstone and so should the top of the tee if it's rough, because the slightest friction that impedes the smooth traverse of the chaser can spoil a thread.

THREAD-CUTTING PROBLEMS

Another problem for thread cutting enthusiasts is the use of poorly seasoned wood so that, having cut a fair thread on a box, it warps in a short time and is therefore unscrewable.

This difficulty is not confined to boxes with screws, as even a push-fit one will need to be loosened if it warps. These are snags we all face, as it isn't always possible to know if seasoned wood is being used.

The seasoned turner, I may say, usually preserves a stock of seasoned stuff, and I don't know a reliable solution except to beg a bit from a friend.

Most of us don't like parting with our valuable old stock but, like gardeners, we enjoy swapping bits and pieces over a friendly visit or a club meeting.

If you do this, be sure to mark the name of any unusual wood, as you're sure to forget it and be back to square one. And someone always asks, 'What wood is that?' Blessed if I know!

I particularly recall a day's visit I had from Hamish Chart, of Reading. To repay me for occupying most of the day he brought me about 33lb. (15kg) of assorted, well seasoned, exotic hardwoods – a delightful gift.

Of course, the plastics don't warp and neither does ivory, bone, horn etc. Once the screw cutting bug has bitten, it's hard to resist

A delightful gift.

the temptation to make screw joins and chance it. In any case, it puts glue well and truly in the shade.

One trouble with chasing I must mention. If you've been using a coarse chaser and afterwards have occasion to use a fine one, you must slow down the speed of traverse, because a fast traverse on a fine thread may produce a double start thread.

This doesn't matter a lot in your own workshop, but dammit! I did it at a demo – at my age! Still, it'd be rather a bore if we got everything perfect all the time – and 'clever dicks' will never be popular.

AVOIDING WASTE
Now, when I'm turning choice hardwoods, from 1⅛–3in (30–75mm) diameter, in a cup

chuck, the piece left in the chuck, perhaps from ¼–½in (6–12mm) or more thick, is something I value. The turner will find a good use for almost anything. So it's annoyingly wasteful when you come to knock it out of the chuck with a stout drift from the back and the prized disc breaks in two.

With larger diameters, I use a screever (thin parting tool) on the armrest and slice it out with a diagonal cut as close to the edge of the chuck as possible.

For smaller, but still useful diameters, I slip a metal disc inside before driving the wood into the chuck. This takes the impact when tapping the enders out and saves breakage.

ACCUMULATION
Discs and enders of various materials (ivory is the best) accumulate slowly, and I've found that whatever is wanted can usually be located in one or other of my many boxes.

My workshop is, of course, a terrible untidy place, but doubtless, I could clear it out if I had a month to spare. And what would happen then? I'd have lost all my useful stock in trade and be ill-equipped to do anything useful. When I clear a bench, the next job fills it again, so I do it only when necessary. Many spend so much time sweeping and clearing up they never find time to make a mess.

To clear a turner's shop, one must hold an inquest over every single item before discarding anything. I find that when I throw something out simply because it's been unemployed for 20 years, I live to regret it.

Some of my most valuable things have been sacrificed to the God of tidiness. No more! The inexorable march of clutter until one becomes totally submerged is, perhaps, only counteracted by moving house every 10 years – and these days that's impossible.

It's too late for me – I'm lumbered in every sense of the word. Yet occasionally, time, an unusual influx of energy, or the imminent arrival of someone I have failed to dissuade from calling (I've mislaid my stout cudgel) finds poor old Bill working like a galley slave clearing up his shop for a day or two. The result, to the visitor, may reveal a chaotic, cluttered turning shop, but to me it sparkles anew, if only for a week. Some people love seeing junk (providing it's someone else's).

A well-known watercolour painter came across an ancient barn, chock full of old farm paraphernalia and junk. It was so congested it had a beauty all its own. He sought out the farmer and explained he had some friends who would love to sketch and paint it if the farmer would allow them to come tomorrow.

The farmer was surprised, but readily agreed, and next day the brothers-of-the-brush duly rolled up, complete with painting gear. When the barn doors swung open, you could've knocked 'em down with a feather. That worthy man had cleared *all* the loverly junk and swept and garnished the whole bloomin' place. You couldn't imagine a more unpaintable subject.

Well, that story's cheered me up, and I shall use it to prevent me from doing anything drastic in the clearing line in the near future. In any case, there's a preservation order on the cobwebs.

GOING OT

A transatlantic reader has asked me if an ornamental lathe he has been offered by an English firm for a fairly high figure would be a sound investment? It's an impossible question to answer. For anyone seriously contemplating ornamental turning, there's a whole new world of turning to learn.

As a hand turner with few engineering capabilities, I'll tell you what I should need for the figure quoted:

1 A basic ornamental lathe with traversing mandrel complete with star wheel, screw guides and chasers to match. Division plate and index. Segment apparatus. Glass hard bearings – sound. Bench with treadle gear.

Ornamental slide rest with horizontal cutting frame.

2 Ornamental slide rest, 12–14in (305–356mm).
3 Overhead gear.
4 Ornamental chucks, viz ellipse, eccentric, rectilinear, dome (or spherical), self-centring, and the usual cup chucks.
5 Cutting frames, viz horizontal, vertical, universal, eccentric and internal. Drill spindle.
6 Small tools and drills for above.
7 Spiral apparatus with Atkinson's reciprocator, plus curvilinear apparatus.
8 Goniostat for sharpening. Brass and steel grinding cones. Slide rest tools etc.

That's my idea of a reasonably complete ornamental turning outfit and has to be worth at least the price of a very good car by virtue of its rarity value and the fact that it's a master-piece of engineering, not made on an assembly line (possibly by robots – human and otherwise).

The snags arise when incomplete lathes are offered to people who have no means of obtaining missing parts, without which no ornamental turning can be done. Even in the Society of Ornamental Turners, ornamental turning equipment is very thin on the ground.

Beautiful cutting frames that used to change hands for a few pounds, now go up to hundreds because they come out of their hiding places so seldom. Even a goniostat, vital for sharpening the tiny tools, can cost £150, and is rarely seen.

So, a complete outfit as listed here can only be priced on the same basis as a rare work of art. It's a matter of negotiation between seller and buyer. As far as I'm concerned they are not museum pieces, but are for use by enthusiasts.

Money has caused good lathes to be vandalized, when chucks made specially for them have been sold off piecemeal to make small lots at auctions.

The unequipped bare lathe, sans chucks, sans slide rest, sans screw guides etc., is worth peanuts because it's of no more value than any plain lathe.

The reader who has been asked for a substantial sum for an ornamental lathe would do well to get a guaranteed inventory and an assurance that *no* essential parts are missing, because they are irreplaceable.

What about the turner who aspires to a modest stab at ornamental turning? What are his minimum needs? Any old lathe (good bearings essential), division plate and index, overhead gear, ornamental slide rest, cutting frames – whatever he can find, especially Universal and Eccentric – drill spindle and drills, small tools, and goniostat.

Even without access to engineering, any turner should be able to contrive his own overhead gear, small tools and even goniostat. The Society of Ornamental Turners (SOT) and/or Christie's, the London auctioneers, should be able to obtain the cutting frames and slide rest.

An advert in *Model Engineer* may also provide what you want. If you are a keen enough hunter, you will most certainly wind up doing some ornamental turning. I did it easily, and although it's vastly more difficult today, it's *not* impossible.

With regard to OT, which can be splendid, outré or just ghastly, I found a fitting sentence by that most erudite of turners, Tobias Kaye: '. . . with any complex technique it demands a high degree of artistry to overcome the impression that the item has been made purely as a technical exercise.' Personally, I'm very sparing with my ornamental turning.

Chapter 14
Copenhagen/Tulip Chess Set: PAWNS

*S*ome people are natural designers with an artistic flair which, by its popularity, ensures success. Some just aren't designers so they wisely leave it to others. I belong to this category and am so accustomed to following established designs or making adaptations to existing patterns, that I seldom attempt to be an original artist simply because I know my limitations.

Yet once in my life I made an artistic adaptation of a chess set which, in several features actually broke into originality and 'knocked 'em sideways'.

> ### BY NOW, in my enthusiasm, I'd forgotten I wasn't a designer – a lapse we can all benefit from

It was an old ivory set I made in '87, from material found in the antiques trade. The competitions arranged by the Worshipful Company of Turners at Apothecaries' Hall, London, that year, included the Lady Gertrude Crawford medal for ornamental turning.

Chess is usually my first choice of subject for although G. B. S. has described the game as 'a foolish expedient for making idle people believe they are doing something clever,' on the other hand Bill Jones has averred, 'Chess is an inspiring and perennial delight to the lathe artist, who need never be stumped for something exciting to make. Those who see chess merely as a game miss the whole point and purpose of its derivation – it was clearly invented by a turner!' But I couldn't imagine a set within my capabilities good enough to enter an ornamental turning competition in just six weeks time. Walther Bach, my friend and colleague in Kent, a chess connoisseur, sent me samples of Lund sets and also photos of a set with a tulip shape in the lower half, together with his keen encouragement.

GERMINAL DESIGN
This occurred on 13 May, '87, when I wrote in my journal, '. . . but I don't think much of them! In the afternoon though, an idea came to me. I amalgamated the spindly Copenhagen set with the lower portions of the tulip set in Walther's photo. The result, after two hours sketching, makes me extremely enthusiastic. If I could make them by 3 July, it would be

Left *Three pieces from 'Old English' chess set.*

terrific! We'll have to see . . .'

I consulted with Walther over the next few days. He was vastly impressed with my sketches, and between us we concocted a design about which he said: 'If it turns out only 50% as good as we hope, it'll be a winner.'

I must explain that the Copenhagen set illustrated in the book, *Chessmen*, by Frank Greygoose, is an ivory one made by J. A. Schwartz of Copenhagen in 1850, *but*, only the king, queen, knight and pawn can be seen. Although I've long admired it, the set is a bit spindly for my taste. Yet, by replacing the lower stems with tulip shapes, they could be magnificent. Four formidable obstacles remained:

1 A more suitable knight, double-headed if possible.
2 A marvellous and original pawn.
3 A rook to complement the high standard of the other pieces in style and prominence.
4 A new bishop, as good as the rook.

By now, in my enthusiasm, I'd forgotten I wasn't a designer – a lapse we can all benefit from. Never say you *can't* do a thing, because you may be right.

Given the circumstances and the zeal, each one of us can rise to heights we'd always thought were beyond us. Stashed away in the brain of an experienced turner are myriads of

Tentative sketches, with poor rook.

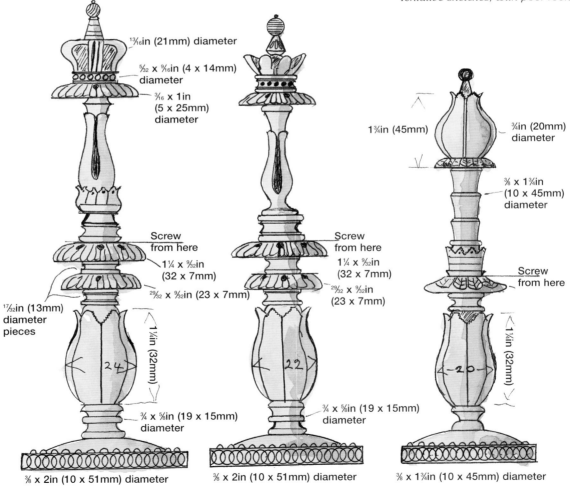

13/16in (21mm) diameter

5/32 x 9/16in (4 x 14mm) diameter

3/16 x 1in (5 x 25mm) diameter

Screw from here

1¼ x 9/32in (32 x 7mm)

17/32in (13mm) diameter pieces

29/32 x 9/32in (23 x 7mm)

1¼in (32mm)

¾ x 5/8in (19 x 15mm) diameter

⅜ x 2in (10 x 51mm) diameter

Screw from here

1¼ x 9/32in (32 x 7mm)

29/32 x 9/32in (23 x 7mm)

¾ x 5/8in (19 x 15mm) diameter

⅜ x 2in (10 x 51mm) diameter

1¾in (45mm)

¾in (20mm) diameter

⅜ x 1¾in (10 x 45mm) diameter

Screw from here

1¼in (32mm)

⅜ x 1¾in (10 x 45mm) diameter

shapes turned at some time or other, and these can be used in a series of sketches and doodles until something appears that provides the basis of the perfect design we seek.

The sketch is just the start. It's in the turning that the design is perfected. After seeing my rough sketches, Walther had a good idea I adapted forthwith, to wit, putting a pattern around the rims of all the bases, plus a row of hemispheres (pearls) around the top of same.

SEPARATE PARTS

All I needed now was time, and I had a fortnight's other work to finish before I could begin. I began on 26 May, spent 30 days and a total of 144 hours on it, and had the set finished by 26 June, but I had to alter my schedule by working a good hour before breakfast. I never enjoyed a job so much or kept up so consistent and sustained a zeal to the almost total exclusion of everything else. At the end, I felt

I'd done my finest ever work. There had been only one hiccough, as you'll see . . .

I'd intended making patterns for the whole set before cutting, but, having started, didn't stop. I'd rough-drawn all the pieces on squared paper, as shown below, showing each piece full size, with joins etc.

I spent 10 hours cutting on the 7in (178mm) circular saw. Ivory, of course, is not a *sine qua non* for such chess sets: some dense hardwoods can be substituted.

The reason so many separate pieces are used (12 parts go to making just the king) is two-fold. First, nothing is wasted with valuable material, we never turn large diameters down to small when a smaller can be joined on.

Second, we often need to work upon the separate parts individually where, in the solid, the same work would be almost impossible. While wood is nowhere near as costly, it's still necessary to retain most of the joins to enable

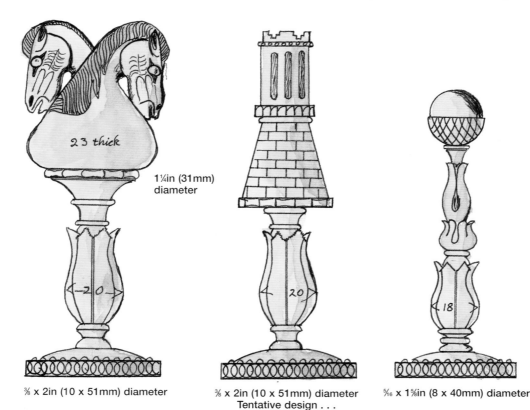

23 thick

1¼in (31mm) diameter

20

20

18

⅜ x 2in (10 x 51mm) diameter

⅜ x 2in (10 x 51mm) diameter
Tentative design . . .

⁵⁄₁₆ x 1⅝in (8 x 40mm) diameter

the special work to be accomplished.

Further, when each part is separate, a superior job can be made of the finishing and polishing, which is a vital part of any work if one is hoping to make something worthy of notice.

PAWN TULIPS

From 7–9 June, I spent 39 hours making 17 pawns. I made one extra of each piece so that at the end I'd have a full set of patterns for the showcase, in case I wanted to make more.

Before beginning, all parts to be turned were hubbed round at the ends on my big cutter. Starting with the pawn tulips in the three-jaw, I turned the tops and drilled and cut the inside threads with a ¼in (6mm) x 26 plug tap, making a true and accurate bed of measured diameter for the stem to screw down upon in true alignment.

First turning of tulips.   *Finished tulip.*

By reversing on a screw plug in the three-jaw, the other end of the tulips were finished to accurate, uniform length and shape, then drilled and tapped with the same tap.

Vee cutter.

There are six vee points at the top of the tulips. I wrote in my journal: 'I try the Holtz for ornamentation, Not a ha'p'th o' use! I had to do them as usual, by hand, with a vee cutter in the three-jaw, and they came out lovely.'

The six points were easily marked out in pencil from the chuck jaws. The vee cutter perfects the points and incises the lines from north to south.

They run dead true, following the curve of the tulip from the bottom of each vee.

Each tulip was held on a length of screwed rod. The tee rest, well back, gave a steadying support for the wrists, and without the smallest wobble or deviation the lines appeared true, like magic.

This sounds more difficult than it is, as five minutes' practice will confirm. Even a sharp and knowing eye would find it hard to detect I hadn't used the curvilinear apparatus. Yet had I used it, the work would not be a whit improved, but it'd be goodbye to hopes of finishing the set in under three months.

The operation, carried out step-by-step on all pieces, speeds up and improves repetition work, and ensures uniformity. I polished all tulips on the buff, which seals the grain, lessens the chance of cracks appearing, and makes another job less to do.

PAWN BASES

Next, I turned 17 pawn bases in the three-jaw. You get a firm and bruiseless grip if you use the outside jaws of a 3in (76mm) three-jaw. I drilled a shallow hole with a D-bit, and tapped and chased the inside threads ⁵⁄₁₆in (8mm) x 26.

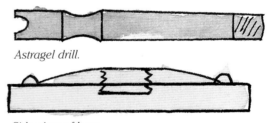

Astragel drill.

Side view of base.

The top of the base was carefully turned, and I made the bead with the flat astragal drill in a socket handle, the same drill I planned to use in the drill spindle to cut the pearls.

Thorough papering, with three grades down to 400 wet-and-dry, was followed by the application of Brasso on cotton wool, which beautifully polishes where a buff can't reach.

Each base was then reversed in the three-jaw to face the bottom cleanly. I went over to my Holtz Eldorado, where I also had a 3in (75mm) three-jaw, to grip the bases for cutting the pearls, but I buffed them as usual, because you cannot do it after ornamental cuts have been made without impairing crispness, the hallmark of good ornamental turning.

With the slide rest at right angles to the lathe bearers, I set up the drill spindle with the re-sharpened astragal drill adjusted to fit precisely over the bead.

Fixing the index on the 144 row of holes, I carefully cut the first pearl and adjusted the depth stop. A little trial and error enabled me to decide on the number of divisions that would provide a pleasing distance between the pearls – too close and they could be damaged, too far apart and unsightly chunks might be left.

The arrangement I settled for, which looked most attractive, did leave tiny columns standing between, but these were easily removed by hand, with a sharp tool.

I used the automatic counting device, home-made from the late G. A. Grace's instructions, which helped things go at a gallop, but although you can go very fast, speed is only possible when you've got everything going to your complete satisfaction and there's nothing to stop you. If you rush it, work may be spoiled.

Now came the barleycorn pattern around the circumference of each base. Another screw adapter plug supported them in the three-jaw.

Barleycorns.

As every turner knows, there is oft a diffi-culty in getting things running true. You can easily tap the plug till the rim of the base runs true, but often the face is a leetle on the slant, so that it wobbles as it revolves. Unless very slight, this is unacceptable.

Then it can be corrected by unscrewing the base and slipping a trifle of paper under one side until, by trial and error, it's near as dammit – that's egzackly!

With a bead drill set to a depth of 1mm or so, I found that 72 cuts (every second hole of the 144 row) achieved nice barleycorns. With my inimitable variable speed, I could make superlative cuts at a very slow speed, raising the foot pedal for each adjustment of the index, getting into an easy rhythm and a speed of 16 cuts a minute.

Bead drill.

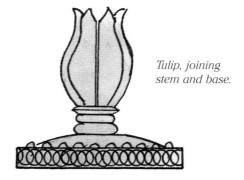

I said ornamental turning cuts are not buff polished, but I make an exception with pearls, as there are no edges or corners and a judicious buffer can really make them sparkle. Pearls are one of my favourite decorative effects.

JOINING BASE TO TULIP

Joining pieces between base and tulip brought them to this stage, sketched below, in a couple of hours. The screw to fit the base was cut first, the shape turned accurately, and the shank for the tulip screw left plain. When every base was fitted with its screw, the tulip screw was cut, while its base was gripped in the three-jaw, so the chances of the whole

Tulip, joining stem and base.

being in accurate alignment were high.

The pawn stem was begun in the three-jaw, by chasing the thread to fit the tulip and tapering the adjacent bead, which made it screw home as snugly as a cork in a bottle.

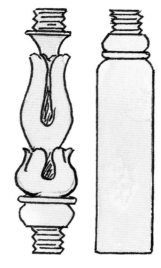

Pawn stem.

To turn the stem in perfect alignment I fixed the base, with its tulip, in the three-jaw and, with the stem screwed home, marked a pencil point at the centre of the other end while it was revolving. I did the same with each pawn. Next, the stem shape was carefully turned between centres, using a tapped plug into which the stem was screwed and gripped in the three-jaw. I centred the other end with a dead centre on the pencil point. I could have used a live centre, but prefer not to.

Round nose drill.

In turning these tight little shapes in hard materials, you gather a number of small tools. The triangular point tool is a must, then several round nose tools, from ³⁄₆₄in (1mm) upwards, a couple of quarter-round tools, left and right, oblique tools left and right, quarter-hollows if you care to make them – all from small files or whatever you can find.

They are easily ground to shape, but are not used straight from the grinder, being nicely honed on a medium India stone or its equiv-

alent, The only one not honed is the hollow ground point tool.

When all stems were turned, I set up the drill spindle in the slide rest and, using a small, round-nose drill, cut four flutes on the upper part, beginning at the middle where the diameter was largest, and ending where the quarter-hollow began.

BUT, sez I, a plague on pernickety persons who would take up microscopes to fault find. All mine are guaranteed slightly different, and that's how I like it

The straight flutes nearly disappeared, most attractively, at the narrow part, Four flutes were then made on the cup, from the meaty part to the top of the cup, but these flutes were positioned midway between the top flutes.

The ornamental turners' slide rest is equipped with fluting stops, so the distance of travel required can be precisely duplicated on each piece: with depth stops to ensure the exact penetration.

It's the work of a moment to unscrew one stem when the top part is fluted and do the same on all stems, then the fluting and depth stops are re-set to flute the cups, and all will finish the same. There is, of course, a proviso. We are fluting hand-turned work, and hand work varies slightly. So, as you find the odd variation, it will be necessary to adjust things as required.

But, sez I, a plague on pernickety persons who would take up microscopes to fault find. If they demand things precisely alike, which is against nature, let them put up with mouldy old moulded work. All mine are guaranteed

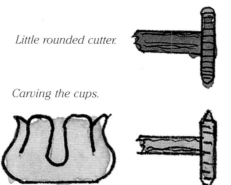

Little rounded cutter.

Carving the cups.

slightly different, and that's how I like it.

In the absence of ornamental turning apparatus, a little home-made rounded cutter, revolving at high speed in the self-centring chuck, will enable the same job to be achieved by hand. Pencil in the lines in the appropriate places, and delicately run the stems down the cutter by hand and eye. Practise on waste first, to be sure you'll get it right, On the cups, between the flutes, I made short incisions by hand with a vee cutter. The tops of all the flutes were rounded like petals, using a dental burr.

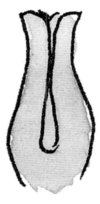

The flute tops are rounded with a dental burr.

ACORN TOPS

I made the acorn tops next, drilling and tapping them ⁹⁄₁₆in (14mm) x 26. A rod was made and a thread turned on the end, to support the acorns while I used a vee cutter to run up slanting chequered lines marked in pencil.

Acorn top.

Although apparently done so crudely, to the not-too-critical eye the resultant pattern was not half bad, I must say. To cut the stem threads to fit the acorns, I wrapped sandpaper and thin leather around them, trued them in the three-jaw with my magic hammer, and chased the threads.

It's permissible to use a die or even a dab o' glue, if your conscience will allow, and you hide the traces. The thread used for the bottom of the stem was ¼in (6mm) x 26 and that for the base ⁹⁄₁₆in (14mm) x 26.

A clever bit of buffing on the 8in (200mm) calico mop, with Cannings Lustre (afterwards brushed out of the incisions with hot soapy water and a toothbrush), caused me to write in my journal, a bit dampeningly '. . . they'll pass! Olive, my wife, passed them, so they must be OK.' And that's half the set.

Chapter 15
Copenhagen/Tulip
Chess Set: ROYALS

Continuing my adventure with the Copenhagen tulip chess set, I began the royals, the three kings and three queens, including patterns. They occupied seven days.

The large tulips and bases went as easily as the pawns. The only difference between king and queen was that the diameter of the queen tulip was ³⁄₃₂in (2mm) less than the king.

MID-SECTIONS

The shish kebab mid-section of carved flanges and distance pieces I described as 'a most engrossing conglomeration of carved and screwed sections that went perfectly'. But it wasn't quite as simple as that.

First, I made the middle carved flanges (six

The large tulips and bases.

Left *Three pieces from French gallery chess set.*

large and six small), drilling and tapping ⁵⁄₁₆in (8mm) x 26, turning them on a screw plug in the three-jaw, and drilling the holes (eight on the large and four on the small). I did it on the Holtz with division plate and index, but, bless yer, hand drilling by eye would have done as well. The carving was done with vee cutters, by hand, clamping each cutter in the three-jaw, the narrow one first, followed by the obtuse one.

Each finger was rounded at the ends by cutter, and to smooth and blend the whole, I finished on a 120 grit flap wheel. Run at high speed, these are quite useful for this kind of job.

A little time spent scraping each finger with a small inside tool will repay handsomely and might well be a deciding factor between a winner and an 'also ran'.

The distance pieces were turned next, taking care to get them exact, six for below the large flanges and six deeper ones for below the smaller ones.

RODS

Now the long screw for the kings. I usually turn all my cut lengths into rods between centres, then clamp the appropriate piece in the three-jaw, chase the 26 thread, or run a die up it.

When striking these long 'uns, I find it easier to avoid inebriated threads by striking at a lathe speed of 1,500–2,000rpm. You don't need to slow down until you approach the shoulder.

Always finish a screw gently, with the chaser below centre, and even on softer materials the tendency to crumble will be averted, 'for the soft

> ## 'I CAN'T do that,' some will say, but you can if you refuse to accept second best. If it doesn't go right, try again until it does!

answer turneth away wrath,' if you follow me.

Having got a good fit and screwed the flanges and distance pieces on, turn the bottom piece to fit the inside of the tulip top and, with a little judicious fitting, a true and successful join is accomplished.

'I can't do that,' some will say, but you can if you refuse to accept second best. If it doesn't go right, try again until it does! As G. K. Chesterton would say, 'If a thing's worth doing it's worth doing badly,' but *not* when I know I can do better.

Sharpening a tap.

In fitting the flanges etc., one or other may prove tighter than the others and should be eased by running the tap through. Here's a good tip for those who use taps frequently until they get dull. Sharpen the leading edges carefully, either with a slip stone or, as I do, on a little grindstone.

The screw will benefit from being polished, because some chess fiends insist on unscrewing all possible and impossible parts of chess – don't ask me why. Further, all parts have to be turned to accurate lengths to avoid variations in the overall height of like pieces.

The upper part of the long screw is turned next, gripping the screw, protected by abrasive paper, in the three-jaw. The cup at the top is bored and tapped to receive the fluted section, then the rest of the shape, down to the large flange, is turned.

I don't need (I hope) to remind you that all these delicate turnings are done with small home-made scrapers, so we're *not* fooling about trying to rub bevels, or buying costly tools that are entirely inappropriate for such work. We are not actually scraping though, because we're not using softwood.

The eight crenellations are cut by hand, with

The Vandyke cutter used for crenellations.

a vee cutter made especially for Vandyke vees, by turning a series of rings on each side of the vee before filing the teeth. A small, plain vee cutter is used to run lines down as illustrated above, and a tiny drill at the top, between the lines, adds a decorative touch.

I found the best way to get the fluted section, which screws into the cup, in true alignment, was to screw the cylindrical piece firmly home (after completing the carving of the cup), and then to turn it between centres.

The rounded tops of the flutes were contrived with tiny cutter and file, exactly like the pawns.

KINGS' CROWN

15 June: 'Early start for a thrilling day on royals. The exacting operation of hollowing the crowns is well done and the kings look magnificent. Work till 9pm.'

The conglomeration of carved and screwed pieces which make up the king.

The ¹³⁄₁₆in (21mm) diameter rods I used to turn those crowns were gripped in the three-jaw while I turned the exterior, bored and cut the 32 thread (a really easy thread to cut). I made a little inside tool like that shown above right, and to make sure it went 'thus far and no

farther,' I filed a mark on the top surface. But before the excavation got under way, I marked, in pencil, six precise places around the crown, using the chuck jaws for my guide.

Whenever I want to remove and replace a rod exactly in a jaw chuck, I place a pencil mark bang in the middle of jaw No. 1 (marked with a file on the chuck) on the rod.

Taking the crown out of the chuck, and fixing a slotting cutter in, I sliced into two opposite sides. After replacing the crown in the chuck, hollowing could then be completed, using the special tool upon the armrest (without which I am improperly dressed, as one turner remarked).

The king and queen crowns.

Sketch of crown.

Frequent stopping is necessary both to clear the swarf and to observe the consistency of the wall shape and thickness. I aim for about ³⁄₃₂in (2mm).

Inside tool used for crown.

This is careful work, both to get the inside consistent with the shape of the outside and to avoid turning away the inside threads. Practise first on a piece of spare stuff, or you'll muff it, but when you've succeeded, you'll be as delighted as I was.

After clearing out the inside and running the chaser up the threads, the crown is parted off, and screwed onto a plug in the three-jaw for finishing the top and drilling and tapping a hole for the finial. A flat point tool is then used to make a little vee ring of ⁷⁄₁₆in (11mm) diameter to guide the work which follows.

Now to make six fiendishly cut wedges, using the slotting cutter – definitely a practise first job, but please, *don't* get nervous. The crown is held by means of a screwed rod for firm control. The drawing above right shows the shape we're aiming for. To make sure it's accurate, top and bottom, the crown is presented both right way up and upside down. It's easy to go too far either way.

Slotting cutter.

The six portions left must be about ⁵⁄₃₂in (4.5mm) because a medium vee cutter is next used to incise a pair of lines around each of the six.

It's not necessary to cut out the wedges with the slotting cutter perfectly. That would be a tall order. Concentrate on *not* going too far and spoiling them, leaving the accurate finishing to some neat work with fine files. I keep sets of needles and warding files which often come to my rescue.

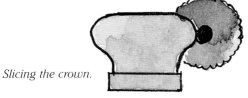

Slicing the crown.

Then, on the Holtz Eldorado, I cut 16 shallow domes around the bottom rim, using a tiny bead drill in the drill spindle. The base of the crown is tapped to screw on the top of the king's stem, and then turned on a plug in the three-jaw, cutting a 32 thread upon which to

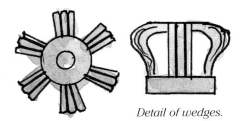

Detail of wedges.

screw the crown, and leaving a hemispherical dome protruding inside, visibly.

This looks splendid when polished. The flange is drilled and carved, the same as the others, and completed with a finial.

Base and finial of the king's crown.

QUEENS' CROWN

The queen (above the long screw) is a bit different, but pretty, and has a different finial to the crown. The three-in-one sketch on page 99 shows how the crown is hollowed, leaving a dome of ⁵⁄₁₆in (8mm) diameter in the centre, level with the top, and drilled and tapped for the finial. Eight shallow holes, made with a ³⁄₆₄in (1mm) drill, are bored at ½in (12mm) intervals around the dome.

The third part of the sketch shows

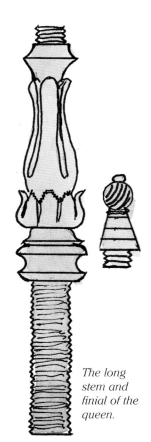

The long stem and finial of the queen.

Constituent parts of the queen's crown.

the slotting saw, about ¾in (20mm) in diameter and ³⁄₆₄in (1mm) thick, as it makes eight radial cuts down to each hole, carefully avoiding mutilating the dome or the top head outside.

I am confident because of my variable speed control and experience, but providing you keep the work on the move to ensure that the saw doesn't bind, you'll find it'll go fine.

With two cutters (slotting and vee) the shapes on the eight sections are negotiated. First, a slot is made halfway down the saw cut followed by the vee which makes them nicely rounded.

Slotting cutter and detail of the queen's crown.

Twelve shallow recessions are made with a round nose drill in the drill spindle, in the bottom hollow.

The carved flange which screws into the crown (but without any dome) is the same as the kings', except that it is ³⁄₁₆in (5mm) thick where the kings' is ¼in (6mm). The polish ensures perfection.

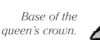

Base of the queen's crown.

BISHOPS

The bishops, rooks and knights (five of each) all had identical bases and tulips, bigger than pawns but smaller than royals. I took 24 hours to complete and polish the lot.

A bishop and rook.

The top six pieces of the bishops, shown in the drawing above (note the difference from the initial sketch), took six hours, just 12 minutes a piece, but I was working against the clock and I have my foot control and armrest, without which I'm a rotten turner.

The tulip, with carved collar in one, was drilled and tapped ⁹⁄₃₂in (7mm) x 26 for the stem and turned on a plug of that size in the three-jaw. I drilled, free hand, eight ³⁄₆₄in (1mm) holes around the collar and slanted the drill to avoid drilling into the top.

I then performed the little 'saw and vee cutter' trick and got a leaf design with a tiny vee cutter so the top of the collar looked like this. This top tulip was crenellated and lined exactly like the large bottom tulips and, with the tiny finial, was quite effective.

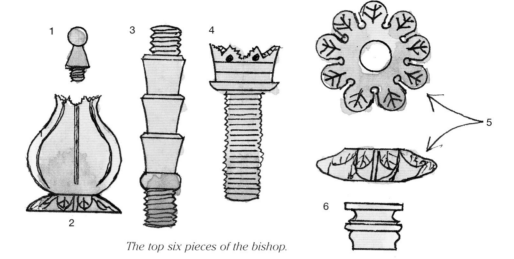

The top six pieces of the bishop.

The bishops' carved flange is shaped differently to all the others. It has the same leaf decoration as that on the collar but with five lines instead of three.

The bishop's top collar design.

KNIGHTS

The five knights took me 17 hours to make. Not bad. I wrote on Monday, 22 June: 'My day's work is on the five double-headed knights. I don't like 'em because I can't reach the mouths with my special 'grinning teeth' cutter, as they have their heads sweetly down upon their chests and tilted a little to one side. But they're going to look all right when finished.'

I normally make my horses grin, or laugh out loud, but this change was necessitated by the limit placed on the width of the two-headed knight.

Next day: 'An early start. A good day, carving knights, which are shaping up, but I still don't know if I'm going to like 'em.'

Wednesday, 24 June: '. . . finally finished the knights, which are rather good and I sneer at those who might consider them top heavy. Only a clumsy person would knock them over, and they can stand it anyway.'

The top part of the two sections between the

tulip and the carved knight was decorated on the Eldorado, with 12 scallops made with an astragal tool in the vertical cutting frame.

The joining section shown at the bottom of the drawing below, is first turned and fitted to the tulip, then the base is secured in the outer jaws of the three-jaw while the other end of the joining section is finished to fit the scalloped piece.

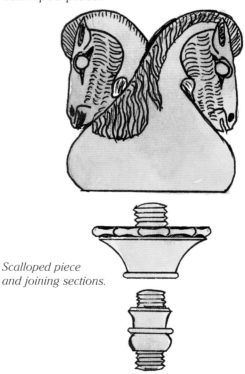

Scalloped piece and joining sections.

Now for the carving. A wide variety of tools can be used for this. Start by pencilling the shape onto each roughly sawn block with a cardboard template.

The large hub is used for getting the thickness of body and heads, and quite a lot more. Two holes are bored through where the neck comes and you simply beaver away with the cutter that presents itself as being most suitable at the time.

Coming to the fine detail, straight and round scrapers, files and glass cloth, bring the work steadily to completion. I was on my own when I carved my very first knights and although they were crude, mainly because I hadn't a good model to copy, they ended good enough to evoke no criticism when I sold them.

It's important to do whatever you do on all the knights before going on to the next stage. Then, if they don't turn out as well as you hoped, the fact they look alike is a virtue that will be appreciated.

Take great care with eyes, ears and mouth and scrape the body beautifully smooth. Try to put character in the mane with the fine vee cutter and I believe you will be quite proud of your knights. Indeed, every time you look at the characterless rubbish they call knights on cheap sets, you will see the difference and enjoy yours the more.

ROOKS

Thursday, 25 June: 'On to the rooks, but the delicate fluted castellations I'd hoped to copy from an illustration in Holtz Volume 5 don't work, which makes me frightfully cut up. I find some of the attractive

pieces of work in that tome are so poorly or incompletely explained that frustration is the inevitable result of attempting them.'

Mea culpa! I lack the brain power, but Holtz should have made allowance for that, if he was capable of putting things simply. When this sort of thing occurs I'm forced to fall back on my own brains, then I really shine. Aha! I have it. That's why the great man doesn't reveal all his secrets . . . the crafty old genius knew we'd rise to the occasion.

The main towers had been turned. To ornament them I made a brass adapter screw to fit a Holtz brass chuck. These useful chucks can have as many adapters as you need. With their help, each piece of work may be returned to the chuck as often as required, so repetitive pieces like chessmen can be managed simply.

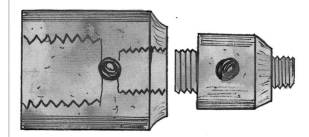

Brass adapter chuck.

Carving burrs and cutters.

The parts which make up the rook.

The adapter chuck is especially useful when several instruments and/or lathe settings have to be employed on a number of identical pieces.

Each operation is carried out on all pieces, then they can all be returned to the chuck accurately for subsequent operations, so avoiding continuously resetting for each piece. What's more, being small, the cutting frames can approach closely without the obstacle of a large self-centring chuck.

Between the top heads of the main tower I made 24 shallow pearls with a bead drill in the drill spindle. I also drilled eight large holes and then connected them to produce the slots, which looked most effective.

The eight cuts around the bottom of the tower were made with a moulding tool in the vertical frame (one of several in my box I hardly ever expect to use). The castellations at the top I made by hand, with a slotting cutter.

The upper towers were then turned to fit into the main towers and as I worked, two brilliant ideas came to me, transforming semi-despair (when the original idea failed ignominiously), to sheer delight!

The first idea was a larger-than-ever carved flange at the bottom of the main tower and, to cap it all (literally), a finial in the shape of a tiny acorn to complement the pawns.

As I set up the slide rest again to decorate the top towers I said to myself, audibly, 'I'm going to enjoy myself scandalous', and I sorted out an LP I hadn't played for years. It was the great Gavioli, a famous Amsterdam street organ that brings tears to the eyes and shatters gloom. That really got things going.

Against all the odds, the set was completed and I don't think a single piece lets it down.

Some 4,500 ornamental cuts have been made and the set has 272 separate pieces.

STAINING

Walther came over on 30 June, with equipment for staining. I used to stain my chess with aniline water dye, but Walther has made an art of it, using all self-procured natural sources.

The colour we agreed was appropriate was horse chestnut. It came out as fine as we'd hoped and, after a rinse and brush, they were laid aside for a day. When glossed on the swansdown mop next morning they were glorious.

Game, set and match.

COMPETITION

3 July, '87: The day of the Worshipful Company of Turners competitions at Apothecaries' Hall, Blackfriars, was an exciting one as usual. The various competitions were well supported and everyone was satisfied. There was a noble display of other work too.

The Copenhagen tulip set was awarded the Lady Gertrude Crawford medal, and Roger Davies, who won a Henry Twentyman medal, stood me a fine mixed grill at an eating establishment in Ludgate Hill.

It was Roger who pulled a wry face as I was unwrapping my set and arranging it on the table as several others were doing. 'We can pack all our stuff away, chaps!' he chuckled dryly. 'Old Bill has won all the prizes!'

Chapter 16
Demonstration DEMONS

Above *Plain boxwood screwed box.*

Demonstrations are always unpredictable! It's amazing how many different snags can arise when you are not in your own turning shop.
As an old scout of Pigeon patrol, I try to 'be prepared', but there are gremlins that I defy anyone to abrogate entirely, crouching, ready to pounce, as you'll later hear.

IMPROVEMENTS

You know my methods. I clamp a $^{29}/_{32}$in (23mm) diameter brass arbor in the three- or four-jaw self-centring chuck provided, and screw thereon a brass cup chuck. The result is slightly juddery, too much so for the item of turnery I had in mind, even allowing for an improvement that had been carried out on the

Harrison Union Graduate shortbed lathe, to wit, the fitting of retractable wheels.

These not only allow this ponderous machine to be handled like a piano, but when in position, can be adjusted to give perfect stability on an uneven floor.

When I first experienced this improvement, I found the lathe (which formerly vibrated slightly) to be steady as a rock. I had a further improvement this time, which was certain to make things even better.

CUP CHUCKS AND CHASERS

I had borrowed an old Harrison mandrel, the nose of which is 1½in (38mm) x 6 teeth per inch, in order to make some boxwood cup chucks to fit. Six is quite a coarse screw tool. I have gathered an extensive array of sizes which, in most cases, cover my needs, but although I found a No. 6 outside chaser I couldn't find its mate, the inside.

My supplier of cheap chasers also failed to find me one. Sheffield provided me with a new HSS No. 6 inside, and the discount price was £28.

Screw-point chuck for making wood chucks.

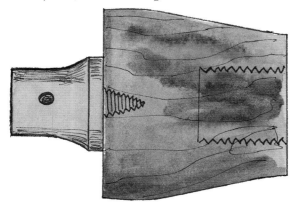

The tragedy was that after I received it, I found a perfect one in another box I'd overlooked. *Mea maxima culpa*! It serves me right, for no hardwood and ivory turner worth his salt ever knocked off to go out and buy a coarse chaser he was only going to use for one

job, even if it did cost him only one shilling and tenpence. And in case someone calculates that as less than 10p, think again, because in those days one could buy seven plates of cod and chips and get a penny change out of one and ten! I should have filed up a chaser to match the nose thread out of mild steel. It would have served as well, or better.

> # REMEMBER, it's the lightness of touch and allowing the tool to cut its own thread, not forcing it to go the way you think it should, that makes for success

I find the outside jaws of the three- or four-jaw self-centring chuck convenient for making wood cup chucks, but it's just as handy to mount them on a screw-point chuck and open the hole, allowing ample room for plenty of practice getting the traverse of the chaser (upon the armrest) right.

Remember, it's the lightness of touch and allowing the tool to cut its own thread, not forcing it to go the way you think it should, that makes for success.

Let your chaser 'flow in' light as a feather, at a good speed of traverse, which you'll get right with practice. The lathe speed can vary from, say, 200 to 700rpm. We can't talk about precision in hand screw cutting.

Precision screw cutting involves exact lathe speeds, lead screws, change wheels and slide rests. We are talking about a 'knack' that can only come with experience, on whatever tackle is available.

Any turner who is determined to cut threads should use offcuts of any good hardwood, turn them into uniform diameter – not exceeding

1⅛in (30mm) – then try making little boxes.

An easy size chaser is 24, but 20 is perhaps the most useful size, the coarser sizes being progressively harder for the beginner. If you make half a gross of boxes out of waste you'll be a screw cutter!

You may end up with firewood or some well-finished and highly polished, saleable boxes – you can do it if you want to. I had a young man who had never turned and yet, after half an hour, managed to make a casein box with a sound screw, plus several duff ones.

But we were chasing a mandrel nose thread. Remove the inside chaser from contact with the work at the end of each traverse because, if you pause a second, that chaser will obliterate

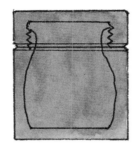

Little box.

the screw. Go too slow and you'll cut a useless double start thread, hence the need to start with a small hole with room to turn away bad work and start again.

'It's dogged as does it!' they say, and you'll find you will conquer this chasing lark and feel the tool travelling up a good screw.

The armrest will no longer feel like a piece of clumsy extra inconvenience you could well do without, but be as natural and unobtrusive as the tee rest. Your left shoulder will, without conscious thought, draw the chaser into cut, applying the appropriate pressure.

You can apply pressure just as soon as you've achieved a sound thread, because it will be the educated pressure of one who has learnt tool control. All you've got to do is believe it.

When you've managed a thread and found it needs enlarging to fit the nose, do not continue with the chaser, for two things will happen. The thread may develop a kink (a drunk thread we call it), or the chaser will go blunt. So you

simply take a little off the thread with an inside tool, leaving half the thread, for we don't want to have to strike a brand new thread again, before continuing with the chaser until a snug fit on the mandrel nose is obtained. Then, skim the face of the chuck so the mating surfaces meet all round with no gaps. All the rest of the work upon that chuck will be done in situ, upon its own mandrel nose.

Ideally, a ring of iron or brass should be fitted to each end so that splitting will be no problem.

The project for my evening demo was a four-piece, screwed, boxwood Staunton chess king. The lathe was wheeled in where I wanted it, someone came and adjusted the wheels and I began.

The chuck clamped in the four-jaw. The wood was chalked and driven in with a hammer.

I used the four-jaw to hold the large cutter I call the 'hub', but when I came to using my new cup chuck, there was no advantage over my former set-up with the brass arbor in the jaw chuck. It was only at the end of the demo that I discovered that the thunderin' wheels had been retracted right off the deck and I never knew it!

The chuck behaved impeccably, but the lathe danced! Still, I managed to make a perfectly acceptable king by using more care than would otherwise have been necessary.

INSPIRATION

But it's not always a Harrison lathe I'm called upon to use, so yet another flash of genius hit the 'little grey cells' recently. Normally there is a four-jaw, geared scroll chuck, with inside and outside jaws. Why not use the stout and positive outer jaws to grip a purpose-built boxwood cup chuck, which would be held as safely and judder-proof as possible?

If a chuck of 2⅜in (60mm) or so diameter were gripped in the outermost jaws, it would be as positive as if the chuck were screwed on the mandrel nose, and the jaws would be well out of knuckle range.

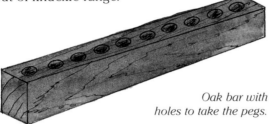

Oak bar with holes to take the pegs.

I had an early chance to experiment, because I'd been asked to make sets of pegs to fit into holes in an oak bar. These numbered pegs are known as draw pullers or position finders and occasionally (if individual pegs could be identified like marked cards), 'fiddle-boxes'.

Waste ivory pegs turned between centres. The flats have been filed and engraved (badly).

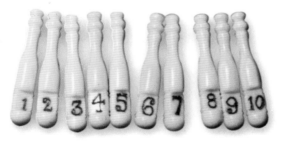

The chap who wanted them had only been able to get nasty moulded plastic pegs, so when he got my samples turned from ancient waste ivory, beautifully made and polished, he was highly delighted. I made him a set of 10, which fitted into a screwed boxwood box.

The holes have been drilled just deep enough for them to fit snugly.

The finished box.

TEST RUN

To make the box I centred a chunk of boxwood in the four-jaw and turned the end carefully, with an infinitesimal taper, so that it fitted into the cup chuck no more than ⅛in (3mm).

I gripped the cup chuck quite firmly in the four-jaw and drove the piece in with my short-handled, 1½lb. (680g) ball pein hammer. I chalked it well and didn't slam it violently, as

A chunk of boxwood centred in the four-jaw.

that could have bounced it out and the lathe might not have liked it.

If you try this, a well directed series of driving blows (spinning the chuck each time to ensure your light opening blows are centring the wood) will culminate in the *coup de grâce*, as the final blow 'whangs the jolly old nail over the crumpet', as it were, and you know by experience that it won't come out of the chuck.

Having said that, I must also add that it will if it wants to. The first over-confident thrust of the gouge at my very first demo sent my wood flying over someone's left shoulder and had the audience backing off hurriedly. I applied that gouge very correctly the next time. Once the roughing out is done, all is plain sailing.

Someone is asking, why not dispense with the services of a cup chuck altogether? I often do, and frequently. But the cup chuck can be tightened more firmly in the four-jaw than you would tighten the actual workpiece.

Also, you have 2–3in (51–76mm) of extra safety margin from the jaws. Once the chuck is in position, you can drive in your workpiece and know it is safely held on the whole of its circumference, rather than on just four parts.

The making of my fiddle box proceeded like

any other. I hollowed the deep lid to the depth decided upon by a rough drawing, then cut the inside thread: No. 20 is my favourite.

I finished the inside with three grades of abrasive paper, then waxed on 0000 steel wool. The photo on page 108 shows the hollowed lid and the male thread I'd cut to fit.

The lid was then screwed on firmly and turned, using a ⅜in (10mm) spindle gouge, a square tool, a three square point tool and a ⅜in (10mm) round nose scraper.

I don't think I could make these boxes very well without the armrest, which doubles the efficiency of the scrapers, gives me better work, and obviates the need for excessive skill, hence my admiration for real woodturners and my surprise that so many strugglers fail to avail themselves of an armrest.

THE first over-confident thrust of the gouge at my very first demo sent my wood flying over someone's left shoulder and had the audience backing off hurriedly

I'm not suggesting that those bent on standard woodturning should forsake orthodox tools and methods, but if screw cutting and delicate turning of harder materials is your aim, the most appropriate tools are a *sine qua non*.

Before finishing the bottom of the box, I made a vee with a flat point tool, at the exact diameter I was going to drill the 10 holes for the pegs.

I then transferred the whole thing to my Holtz Eldorado lathe, and with division plate and index, drill spindle and depth screw,

The end is turned to enter the chuck at about ⅛in (3mm).

The hollowed lid, with the male thread cut to fit.

drilled 10 holes to fit the pegs at the precise depth to allow a millimetre play inside the lid. Without the luxury of a Holtz I would, of course, have done it by hand, with no observable difference.

The benefit of the outside jaws is that they each grip about ½in (12mm) of the circumference, whereas the inner jaws are necessarily pointed and are likely to bruise work.

So, using the outside jaws, I gripped the bottom of the box by the male thread, lapped with glass paper to be on the safe side, and, with a square tool on the armrest, I skimmed the base and finished it with two neat vees for appearance, remembering to wax them or the

vees would have shown lighter.

I buff polished and glossed everything and despatched confidently. My client couldn't have been more delighted. This customer came from a referral and shows the value of a good reputation in whatever craft you follow.

DARE TO BE DIFFERENT

But don't just be 'one of the crowd', or you may wait till doomsday and never be noticed. As Ravel said when Gershwin came to him for music lessons: 'Why be a second class Ravel when you can be a first rate Gershwin?'

In short, to succeed be different, as only you can. All you've got to do is believe it!

Chapter 17 ● A
Woodturners' *Gathering*

T he approach of the Association of Woodturners of Great Britain's (AWGB) biennial seminar at Warwick University in August, had me anxiously getting together my bag o' tricks.

For three demonstrations I had to prepare a large tool bag containing about 44lb. (20kg) of tools, timber, tackle, chucks, cutters, hammers, chalk, candle, abrasives, polishing buffs, compo, measuring tools, chasers, armrest, etc.

Having assembled everything, I sharpened the edge tools, stacked them in the bag, fastened it and left the shop. I nearly omitted the measuring tools, which I found all together on a bench, and only just remembered the armrest, without which I am *hors de combat* to begin with. But the seminar was very enjoyable and fully repaid the days of preparation.

I can best describe the event by referring to

Above *The square tool.*

my journal (the shop's log) which I've kept daily for more than half a century. I'm on book number 43 now.

DAY ONE

Friday, 11 August, '95: Really hot! Up at 5.30am for the Warwick seminar. I am travelling there with friends Colin Firth, Alec Owen and Mike Alawi of our club, the Thameside Woodturners' Association.

Colin collects me at 7.50am, we pick up Alec and Mike at Benfleet and, after a pleasant drive, arrive at about 10.15am. Everything looks beautiful and not one building is old. We kept together, or we'd have been lost in no time.

We found our *en suite* rooms superb – a distinct improvement on Loughborough. Judging by the familiar faces of friends and fans there are many who regard this seminar as unmissable.

> THE offerings were wonderful and various. Some were miraculous, others rubbish, and some, marvellous and startling pieces, many of which were, to me, works of genius!

We shunted our exhibits along to the instant gallery, where I saw work of a very high standard being unwrapped. We returned to the Rootes Building, which was sheer opulence throughout, with its spacious reception hall complete with two vast circles of the most comfortable settees, glass coffee tables and snack bar.

Upstairs to lunch in a perfect dining hall – as good as Selfridges – with choice of hot or cold succulent meals and seating room for over 400. Before lunch we had time for an aperitif in the huge, luxurious bar with not a single hard seat in sight.

There was only one demo period on the opening day, from 3.30pm to 5.30pm. As I was free, I elected to give Bert Marsh the pleasure of my company while he tentatively tackled the turning of a wet, natural top, burr bowl – which wasn't easy.

Towards the finish (it was a delicate bowl and 'coming through the side' was a distinct possibility), I suggested he 'tried the gouge that cuts!'. He muttered something that sounded like, 'There's always one!'.

Although two hours seems like a generous allowance for the project, Bert only just managed to finish in time due to the problems of that chunk of wet wood.

I always feel so much better after seeing someone else struggling and I thought, my work is a doddle after that. I guess it's all a matter of what you get used to.

The evening's entertainment was a slide presentation of North American turnings, given by John Jordan. The offerings were wonderful and various. Some were miraculous, others rubbish, and some, marvellous and startling pieces, many of which were, to me, works of genius! John gave us much food for thought on the subject of art and design.

The heat in the lecture hall was fearful, but the bar afterwards was a cool oasis, in which serious turning matters could be discussed with friends old and new, with never a thought or mention of this ludicrous old world from which it is so delightful to escape for a whole weekend.

I was ready for my bed, but would I sleep in such heat? I sat on the bed in *puris naturalibus* writing this entry in my log. Then I made myself a strengthening cuppa and retired.

DAY TWO

Saturday, 12 August: Up very early. Breakfast begins at 7.30am and I can't wait to be 'up and at 'em'! This morning I'll be making a five-piece rattle at 9am. It's an 'all go' job with not the slightest chance of any turner becoming bored! All fear has gone because I have off-loaded self and can only think of what I'm going to give out.

After the traditional English breakfast, I repair to my allotted and excellent workshop, where I soon find the boxwood chuck I made specifically for the Harrison 'Grad' doesn't fit.

Holtzapffel mandrel noses are seldom alike, although I have two that are, which is useful for transferring work half done from one lathe to the other for special jobs! I didn't bargain for Harrison noses to vary.

This was slightly big for my chuck, but fortunately I was 10 minutes early and I was prepared with my No. 6 inside chaser, so quickly fixed the chuck in the outside jaws of a four-jaw, and worked on the threads until the chuck fitted.

I had a good audience and, in spite of several wrong moves, because I forgot to look at my step-by-step instructions, ended with a passable rattle.

Mislaying my middle-sized drill, I was forced to drill larger holes. But I found this improved both appearance and sound, as the bells were louder. It was a great success which did wonders for my confidence.

After my demonstration, I enjoyed the open and instructive walk through the instant gallery with John Jordan, Mike Hosaluk and Paul Clare leading the discussions, but inviting onlookers to participate.

There was so much good work of great variety to examine, and these fine artist/craftsmen taught many of us some extremely useful points in a kind and amusing way. I for one learnt something extra about design.

The word 'lunch' trips lightly off the pen, but 'tis an important function, not only for the toothsome fare, but also for the company. So many friends had a chat with me that a line from Henry V kept coming to mind,

'Gentlemen in England now abed shall think themselves accursed they were not here!'

After lunch, I spent an hour and a half watching Richard Raffan turning a lidded box with impeccable dexterity. This gave me half an hour to grab a cuppa and prepare the next Harrison lathe. The mandrel nose was different again so they certainly don't come out of the same mould.

Prepared as usual, I used my special boxwood cup chuck, secured immovably in the outer jaws of the four-jaw. A goodly crowd watched me turning a 40-year boxwood screwed box, decorating the lid with an old billiard ball ivory flower.

At the trade stands I treated myself to a new grinding wheel and an inside (rattle) tool from Ashley Iles, then tottered back to the billet for tea and to freshen up.

In the evening a banquet was laid on, a sumptuous spread, with wine. We all looked as clean and as sparkling as woodturning delegates ever can!

Len Grantham actually sported a tie, perhaps because he was running the auction. And what an auction! Len's repartee was priceless and, being a charity event, the turned items donated reached high figures. Why, the box I'd just made fetched £95!

To crown the evening, I was invited to join Ray Key, Bert Marsh and others for a drink. The new editor of *Woodturning*, Neil Bell, was there and after an hour Bert button-holed me in a fatherly way, (well, Len Grantham *did* refer to him as the 'Grand Old Man of Turning'!) and began discussing my articles . . .

The gist of his ramblings, and I can't be precise as both of us were the better for drink, was that Bert regretted that he had encouraged me to write for the magazine initially and added: 'It might be a good thing if you took a rest from churning out those boring old notes and sketches for a spell. Never mind about the money.'

Mr Bell didn't agree and looked sympathetic. He told me not to worry and that he'd see me in the morning for a serious discussion.

I was stunned to say the least, at the bare idea of being elbowed onto the scrapheap. This was my first whiff of opposition, having received naught but encouragement up till now. But I'm dog-tired and we shall see . . .

DAY THREE

Sunday, 13 August: The morning after. I think I know what it is! Everybody loves old Bert and his bally bowls. Then he hears nothing but BJ, the wonder man, month after month, and finally he blows his top. But it won't wash. He'll have to put up with it!

The coolness which began last evening continues for another nice day. I'm up early and get my case packed before breakfast. Running into Ray Key, I told him of Bert's outburst and he assured me definitely that Bert was 'winding me up!'

I then ran into Bert, who confirmed the same, taking my arm and asking when my book was coming out. I later learned that a book was to be published in October '95, entitled *Bert Marsh: Woodturner*. He really was winding me up. The rascal!

It was wonderful to go to a breakfast of cornflakes, egg, bacon and sausage, toast and marmalade, orange juice and coffee, to be greeted on all sides with 'Mornin' Bill'.

We cleared our rooms, put the cases in the car and handed in our keys, more than a little sadly. I gave my last demo to an agreeable crowd which included Mike Hosaluk, the Canadian artist/turner. My Staunton king in four screwed pieces was a success and I gave many pointers on screw-cutting, use of point tool and much more.

An old music hall song had caused me sleepless nights, but in the event I had no inhibitions and was entirely at home with my audiences. Do you remember it?

I acted so tragic the house rose like magic,
The audience yelled 'You're sublime!'
They made me a present of Mornington
    Crescent,
They threw it a brick at a time!
Someone threw a fender, it caught me a
    bender,
I hoisted a white flag and tried to surrender.
They jeered me – they booed me,
And half of them stoned me to death.
They threw nuts and sultanas, fried eggs
    and bananas,
The night I appeared as Macbeth!

I chose to watch Gary Rance for the next demo period. He is a great young turner who can't help being popular. When earlier I told him I intended to watch him he said modestly, 'You won't learn anything from *me*!' But I found him a happy demonstrator who was completely at home and of course *did* teach us all something, especially me.

After a superb lunch of roast beef, horse-radish sauce, Yorkshire pud, baked spuds, cabbage, apple pie, custard and coffee, we conveyed my tool bag to the car and I attended the final demo, choosing Mike Hosaluk, to whom I had given my chess king.

Mike was making surface patterns and painting bowls and other items. He insists on plenty of variety in his work and does not duplicate demos – a talented and popular turner.

The final speeches and farewells were a delight. Ray Key, who had done so much in organizing the seminar, (in the sad absence of Tony Waddilove whose illness robbed us all of his exuberant lead) had difficulty in bringing the standing ovation to a close.

THE BJ TRIANGULAR POINT TOOL

A funny thing happened at the Ashley Iles trade stand. I found some round lengths of HSS, about 7 x ⅜in (180 x 10mm) diameter, and immediately thought, 'what excellent Bill Jones triangular point tools they'd make'.

I made one on my return to Ye Olde Dumpe and am now using it. I can say I find it even better than those made with a three square file. It handles better in every way as it rolls and slides over the tee rest so well.

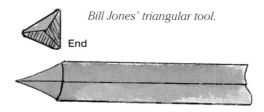

Bill Jones' triangular tool.

The reason three square files were used is that, for a start, they were free and because we always had worn out saw files and used them for point, round nose, inside and every other shape of small tool, including parting tools (screevers).

Should a sudden serious shock occur, such as inadvertently sliding into the chuck jaws, (all things are possible), the file will, of course, shatter. I can't recall a single instance of anything more than a trivial injury caused by a file breaking.

Indeed, if the file did *not* break, the injury might be more serious! However, it is possible a broken piece could damage an eye, so although, personally, I will always utilise files, I

never advise others to. I do advise protective spectacles though.

For three square point tools which are hollow ground to a three-sided pyramid from north to south, the 120° angles are already there, and the grinding is simple. Just hold it up to the top of the wheel, as the drawing below left shows, moving it slightly from side to side and by feel, getting just the one accurate hollow on each of the three sides.

Unless it is continually quenched in cold water you may blue the top which will spoil the tool.

To use round HSS you have to judge the three 120° sides and they take a bit longer to grind, otherwise there is no difference. With the handle, the overall length of the point tool should not exceed 10in (255mm) as the handle has to pass across the solar plexus freely.

I must make a better job of explaining how to manipulate this tool because it has puzzled some who have attempted – and failed. First, forget the bevel completely! We'll have a session to master this easy tool. I will try to sketch the details to make it clear.

THE PLANING CUT

Keep tool slanting as shown below, and the handle well down. The cutting is all done with the right edge. The left edge is raised a little off the work, but there is nothing to catch or dig in as the tool is round, the point is clear of the work and there's no back end to catch at all.

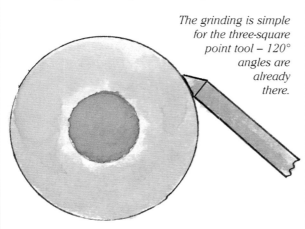

The grinding is simple for the three-square point tool – 120° angles are already there.

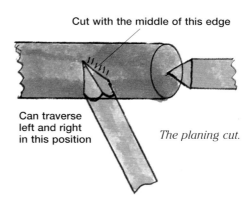

Cut with the middle of this edge

Can traverse left and right in this position

The planing cut.

If your tee rest is rough, it must be smoothed with an oilstone and kept frictionless by frequent rubs with a candle. Your tools will always sail along joyously if you do this. That's why I'm never without a stump of candle in my apron pocket – don't you be.

SURFACING OR CUTTING A SHOULDER

The top face (it has, of course, three faces and you can use any one as top) is almost horizontal, but tilt it slightly to the left and it's the left hand edge that controls the direction of this cut.

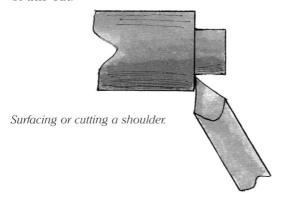

Surfacing or cutting a shoulder.

Experiment confidently, as more dig-ins occur when you are waiting for the worst to happen. Don't worry about the point tool – it's a beautiful 'non-digger.'

ROLLING BEADS

Start as for surfacing, top horizontal, then tilted slightly left. Move the handle down and to the left, twisting the cutting edge downwards as you go.

With the movement of the handle round, you have perfect control of the clean shape of the bead whereas, using a skew, the shape has to be contrived by a wrist movement.

For the left side of the bead, use the same instructions vice versa. Now someone will say, 'Ah, but you are cutting uphill, which ain't done!' This is thinking like a woodturner following rules, and not like a hardwood and ivory turner

who observes the rules, but reserves the right to get on with the work and damn the rules if he likes. But if you feel like that, simply start from the top with the handle down and raise it as you twist it round, downhill.

Rolling beads the easy way.

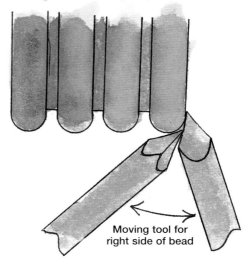

Moving tool for right side of bead

It works, because I've just tried it on a length of softwood, buddleia no less (not many have tried that). I made 16¼in (6mm) deep screever cuts, ⅜in (10mm) apart.

The eight beads on the right I rolled with a ⅜in (10mm) square beading and parting tool ground as a skew, using the long point (which is marginally better than the short).

You can't easily dig in with this most excellent skew, which all tyros should have, as it does most of what a big skew can do and lots that the big 'un can't. And if you doubt that, ask Ray Jones, who is a *good* turner.

The left side eight beads I rolled – four uphill and four down – equally easily using my point tool, and do you know what? Not a ha'p'th o' difference, and all eight were more shapely than those I skewed. I therefore give my unqualified recommendation to all turners: use the BJ round, HSS, triangular point tool.

Chapter 18
Favourite LATHES

*A*ll lathes have their personal characteristics. If you have just one you will get to know exactly what you can and can't do on it. Necessity may well oblige you to attempt something abnormal and you'll manage if you must.

Still, it's a pleasure to have a light one, a heavy one and/or a hollow mandrel, each of which comes into its own at various times.

I was idly ruminating as I tramped o'er the meadows with Guinness, the crossed labrador, recently, that it might be advisable to off-load one or two lathes and surplus tackle. I then mentally examined each one of my six to discover if I had an expendable one . . .

BASHER

The big, 8in (203mm) 'basher' I use for turning, circular sawing, sanding disc, carving cutters, grinding and buff polishing (to mention a few of its manifold uses), has been driven by ⅓HP sewing machine clutch

Above *Turning a boxwood cylinder.*

motor for 45 years. Usually there'll be a convenient overhead beam to which a boxwood pulley can be screwed, but in its absence I've constructed the angle iron set-up shown below, which is bolted to the bench.

Normally such motors are under-slung, but it suits me better to have it behind the headstock so that when tapping or unscrewing I can run the belt back'ards manually.

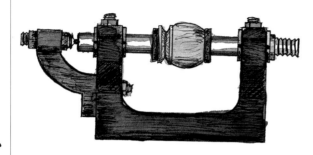

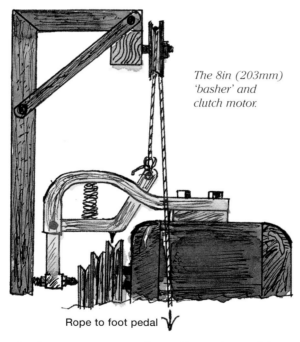

The 8in (203mm) 'basher' and clutch motor.

Rope to foot pedal ⬇

I take any amount of trouble to have things working exactly how I like them, and they're always infinitely adjustable and satisfyingly crude.

My father, Bertram, had fast and loose pulleys on the mandrel when he worked on the basher in the 1930s. The left side one was loose, so

when he wished to stop the lathe he used a tool handle to flip the flat belt over from the fast to the loose pulley and the lathe could then be stopped with a hand on the chuck.

I had a similar machine in a shaving brush factory, where I spent a couple of years before the war, and had lots of two-piece screwed handles to make. The belt from an overhead shafting could be shifted over to the loose pulley, by a simple sliding bracket above the mandrel.

A thumbscrew actuated a sliding fork which moved the belt over. Thus, I could move the belt onto the loose pulley, then move it $\frac{3}{16}$–$\frac{1}{4}$in (5–6mm) over onto the fast pulley, securing it in that mid-position with the thumbscrew.

The partial drive enabled me to obtain the very low speeds necessary for chasing threads and, as the lathe gathered speed, it could be slowed by a hand on the chuck.

I'm sure Bertram found an equally effective way on the 'basher', even without the luxury of a fork. He used it all the while I was with him and passed it on to me in 1947. There were quite a few iron and boxwood chucks and special wood chucks for mirror frames and unusual jobs.

A familiar face on the 'basher', taken in 1961.

I used it for many turning jobs, banging the work into cup chucks in the time-honoured manner. I made many thousands of boxwood catheter plugs, hundreds of peppermills and condiment sets, chairmans' hammers and the like.

The photo, below left, of me working on the basher, was taken in 1961, when I had a turning shop in St.Ives, Cornwall. I seldom use it now for turning, because it's a bit of a rattler (I never knew it when it wasn't) and for cutting threads I've been spoilt by the solid reliability of its adjacent neighbour, the Acorn.

ACORN

Although I have some cup chucks for the Acorn I have, over the years, become so accustomed to the three-jaw, self-centring chuck, that most of the work I used to do with cup chucks I now do in three- and four-jaw chucks, with and without adapters.

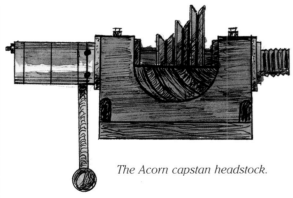

The Acorn capstan headstock.

The reason old turners seldom used engineers' chucks is mainly because they worked with a fixed speed and 'fast and loose' pulleys, with flat belts which jolted over the fasteners. What a life!

It was a revelation to me after the war, when I discovered vee belts: and after fitting them it was like a rest cure. I lost no time introducing them to Bertram, who was equally enthusiastic.

Once you get used to a thing you tend to use it for more and more work. So it was that I became a three-jaw instead of a cup chuck man. Believe it or not, this preyed on my conscience at first – it seemed downright immoral! But, of course, in spite of my forebodings, I never grew rusty in the art of the cup chuck and still often use and recommend it.

I can do almost anything on the sturdy little Acorn capstan headstock, which was 3½in (90mm) centre – raised to 5in (125mm) to match an old tailstock (for most of the old campaigners picked up their bits of lathery where they could). I actually bought the Acorn head, with its timkin taper roller bearings, brand new and it paid for itself in a month of pen work.

Because it's a steady runner at any speed my foot desires, I can control my turning better on her than any other in my shop. It is equipped, as you see, with quick closing collet mechanism.

LARGE CONE

The third lathe, next to the Acorn, on the 12ft (3.7m) bench I bolted together out of old 4 x 2in (102 x 51mm) timber, is the 6in (150mm) hollow mandrel, which will accommodate 1³⁄₃₂in (27mm).

I seldom use it because it isn't a patch on the Acorn. It has a large cone front bearing that tends to bind when a drill is pushed in.

Nevertheless, I'd be lost without her for certain jobs. When I use a light, 2in (50mm) self-centring chuck for turning casein rod and get her going, she soon gets in the mood and runs very well.

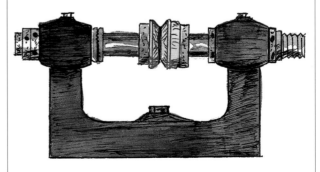

The 6in (150mm) hollow mandrel.

This lathe and the Acorn are driven from a shafting below which is powered by a 1HP motor via a Brammer vee belt. Both lathes have back carriages at the rear, driven by this shafting by a flat slipping belt – a costless variable speed without which I am only fit for stacking planks.

LEG VICE

At the end of the bench I have my big leg vice, with 4½in (112mm) jaws. I've filed up thousands of mouthpieces in that vice when I worked extensively for the pipe trade, and when I consider flat work and carving, my trade without a vice would be almost impossible.

Bertram and I picked it out at Clerkenwell, new, in '48, when he generously provided me with a pretty good start in my first turning shop.

VAMPIRE

We're at the shop door now. It's 18 x 8ft (5.5 x 2.3m) and with six lathes some would find it claustrophobic – to me it's cosy! Opposite the vice stands the Vampire, which consists of an 1813 Holtzapffel and Deyerlein 5in (125mm) headstock, which I bought in the early '50s for just £9.

It has a traversing mandrel for screw cutting and the star wheel is engaged and disengaged from the screw guide by means of a sprung lever, which actuates a thick brass plate to which the star wheel is secured.

I made a solid 5ft (1.5m) bench out of the stoutest old timber I could scrounge (we didn't actually buy timber for such things in our trade), screwed down lengths of 1½in (38mm) angle iron for the lathe bearers, and laboriously filed them as flat as time and patience would allow.

I rigged an angle iron overhead gear, set a ½HP motor underneath, also a countershaft midway on the back members of the bench. The usual back carriage, fixed to the top rear member behind the headstock, gave me perfect, foot-controlled variable speed for both the headstock or the overhead.

I mainly use this famous lathe for organ stops, but it is the first choice for woodturning and many other varieties of work. It is by no means a valuable lathe, except in my affections.

MUCKLE

Next to the Vampire stands a little beauty of a lathe, made by as good a lathe maker as ever there was in the last century – Jonathan Muckle of Monkwell Street, Cripplegate, London.

It's a treadle lathe with cast iron lathe bearers on a splendid mahogany bench, 38 x 24in (97 x 61mm). The lathe is a 5in (125mm) centre, or 42in (104cm) from floor to centre height, which coincides with the distance from floor to my elbow – just right in fact.

A five-drawer cabinet sits beneath the backboard, containing small tools, chucks and screw tools and screw guides or hobs, for this is a traversing mandrel, screw cutting lathe.

It was also a rose engine, but when it came to my notice it was incomplete and, being ill-equipped to attempt to fathom the inscrutable workings of the mind of the long dead maker, I have been content to use this delightful old warrior for plain (but always first class) turning, and especially spindle work.

Having substituted a lignum vee pulley for the huge division plate/rosette pulley, the Muckle is a lively runner so that, like the Vampire, it's a bit skittish for thread chasing by hand, the weight lacking, you see.

Therefore, on the projecting end of the mandrel, I have firmly clamped a discarded 4in (100mm), three-jaw chuck, which steadies the lathe beautifully and gives much better control in speed variation.

When I took the Muckle to Olympia (some years ago) for the DIY exhibition – on Friedlein's natural materials stand – the organisers not only barred this chuck but had the mandrel end boxed in with plywood. Of course they were not concerned with my safety but that of the public: a 4in (100mm) chuck in the ear would've landed us all in the cart.

The treadle wheel abides elsewhere for two reasons:

1 I drive the Muckle with a ⅓HP clutch motor (same as the 'basher'); and
2 I can't stand cracking my shins on treadle wheels in my narrow shop.

I must tell you, this lathe was rejected by an old friend (now deceased) who thought I might like it, as it was only £25. It was transported from Yorkshire to London by Pickfords for 30 bob, in those happy days.

ELDORADO

The last lathe, lying next to the Muckle, was named in all innocence by Bertram, who came into the shop just after it had arrived, and said, 'Let's see this Eldorado of yours!'

It's a fine, near complete Holtzapffel ornamental lathe, first sold in 1844 – a 5in (125mm) screw mandrel lathe, raised to 6in (150mm). I used the treadle to begin with and turned a few dozen two-piece cabinet knobs.

I still have the treadle gear stowed away, but I've motorized it in my own unusual way, as the illustrations here show. Some say the motor should be on the deck, but I have mine (½HP)

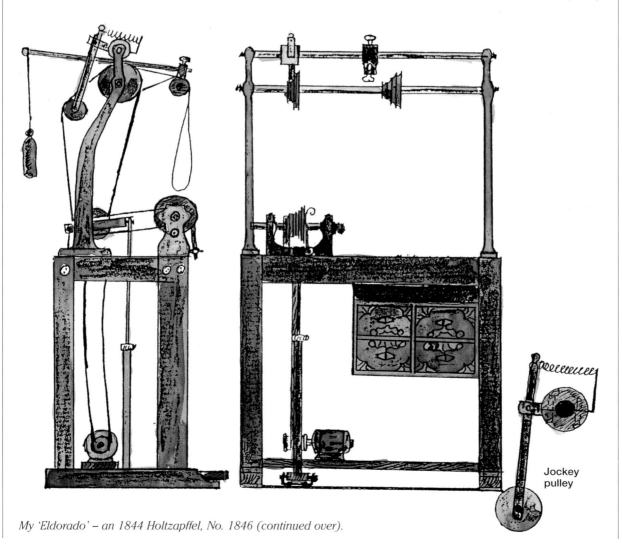

Jockey
pulley

My 'Eldorado' – an 1844 Holtzapffel, No. 1846 (continued over).

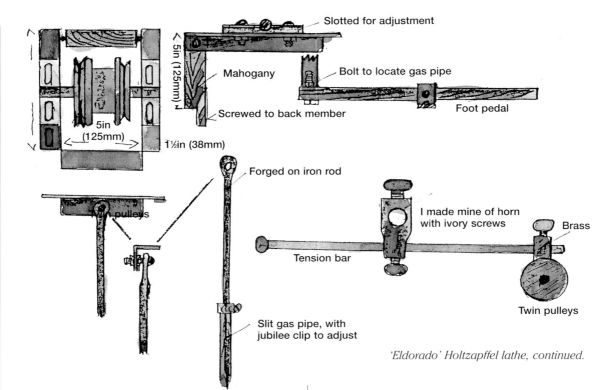

Slotted for adjustment

Mahogany

Bolt to locate gas pipe

Screwed to back member

Foot pedal

5in (125mm)

5in (125mm)

1½in (38mm)

Forged on iron rod

Twin pulleys

I made mine of horn with ivory screws

Brass

Tension bar

Twin pulleys

Slit gas pipe, with jubilee clip to adjust

'Eldorado' Holtzapffel lathe, continued.

mounted on a rubber-cushioned, very stout plank, screwed to the bottom cross members.

The 4in (100mm), flat motor pulley drives the 4in (100mm) flat back carriage pulley via a 1in (25mm) flat leather belt. A 6in (150mm) back carriage vee pulley drives the 4in (100mm) lathe pulley via a ¼in (6mm) round leather belt.

The right-hand, 6in (152mm) vee pulley on the back carriage drives a stepped vee pulley on the overhead, with a jockey pulley midway to take up the slack. The drawings left and above will make it all clear. Everything is fully adjustable and the cost is negligible.

The back carriage is raised and lowered by the foot pedal. The bracket on which the pedal is mounted, is fixed to the iron strip that should be on all treadle lathes right under the foot pedal.

The overhead and lathe can be run separately or together. The driving rope for the cutting frames runs from a moveable, stepped pulley, over the twin pulleys on the tension bar, down to the cutting frame.

It can go as fast or as slow as you want. You often know that an alteration of speed (up or down) would greatly improve its efficacy, and a foot-controlled cutting frame speed, which can pause for every adjustment of the index, is a luxury few know.

Ah, you may say, treadlers know it! All those folk know is that they came into the workshop for a bit of peace and quiet and ended up hopping up and down on one leg. I know one who insists upon it – for the exercise, he says. He wouldn't have it any other way.

The only modification to the sacred Holtzapffel woodwork is a slot cut out of the backboard, about 16 square in (103 square cm), but if that is an objection, the original can be replaced and the old one stored.

The back carriage three-in-one wooden pulley has a boxwood spindle with two old ball races inset. The spindle ends are screwed to slotted boxwood beds, giving ample adjustment.

'Well, Guinness,' I said, 'I ain't gonna part with any of my lathes!' Would *you*?

Chapter 19 ● *Sanders,* Polishers and CUTTERS

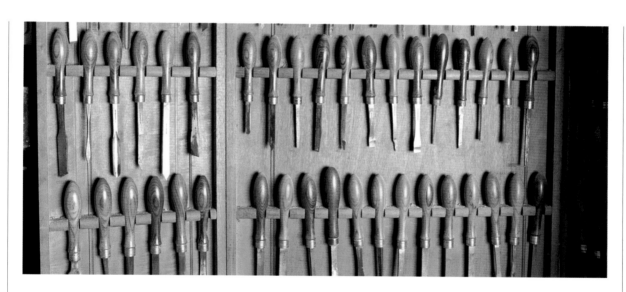

Above   Cabinet of Holtzapffel hand tools with rosewood handles.

There is no finer place for reflections – or, as the late Wilfred Osborne, one of the finest editors of the bulletin of the Society of Ornamental Turners, used to say, 'musings from the mandrel' – than your own turning shop.

I'll begin my ruminations with a letter from a friend in Bristol, who wrote . . . 'in passing, may I say I wish my workshop was as tidy as yours, as shown in the September issue [Issue 35] of *Woodturning*.' What a kind thing to say! I know what he means, as I'm actually able to stand at the lathe in that photo.

RUBBISH TIP

Shops can get so cluttered there's no floor space at all. Parkinson's Law is well founded. What happens is that everything that is not useful or beautiful in the house and might otherwise go to the tip, ends up in the workshop – or the loft.

My loft has a big opening flap, and a ladder I made over 30 years ago, which can be lowered or raised by a rope, two pulleys and some bricks.

As it's a performance taking things up, and a bigger problem finding storage space when I get there, it's difficult to decide if something is so unlikely to be wanted that it should be taken to the loft. But lack of workshop space forces me to continue storing treasures there. Half the items I finally decide must go up are required PDQ (pretty damn quick), but that's another law we all know.

Clearing the shop is a never-ending task, because no sooner do I begin, than everything is cluttered again. When friends drop in it gives them pleasure to see they can't compete with me for untidiness, so I refuse to spoil their delight.

If I do sweep up and dust, so that the lathes can be seen, giving my old shanty the look of an Aladdin's cave – or something like it – then, you've guessed, the guests don't turn up! When they do, the turning shop is in its normal 'orrible state.

Let's look at a job I occasionally received, for several position finders in the shape of engraved flat pegs, in various sizes, about ¹⁄₁₆in (1.5mm) thick. To make them, I cut small blocks from waste that will yield at least two and sometimes four or five. I cut each rectangle on a fine, 7in (180mm) circular saw, a very safe job which would be banned by today's regulations. Strange how the old joke has become a reality – if anyone wants to work, some busybody who doesn't will fight the case!

It's a nice little 20 gauge saw, for which I hand-turned and screwed an alloy arbor to fit the 8in (203mm) 'basher' lathe. I have several small saws between 18 and 22 gauge and 7 teeth per inch, and doctor them myself.

The arbors on two are alloy and the rest lignum. The little saw table is perfect for my work and, although it may appear hazardous, the top speed is 2,300rpm and the foot control boosts confidence.

As you know, I never allow switches to interfere with my work – except when I'm demonstrating and working under the same handicap as the rest.

Once the motor is switched on, everything is done from the foot pedal until knocking-off time.

When I tell you I often have to stop the lathe six or more times a minute, you'll realize how impossible ordinary machines are in my trade.

FRIGHTENING

The idea of a circular saw hissing under my nose with no foot control would frighten me, but there's no regulation against that to my knowledge.

The 7in (175mm) x 20 gauge circular saw.

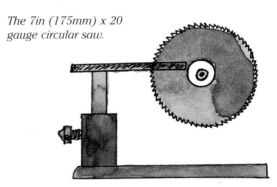

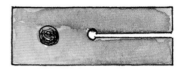

I've been accustomed to sawing very small stuff most of my life, and the only accident I ever had was in a brush factory, when I was using a wooden pusher to advance the work on a pukka circular saw – fortunately only a 12–14in (305–355mm) one.

The pusher slipped off and I jabbed my thumb on the saw. A chair, a cup of tea and a piece of band-aid put me right in 10 minutes. Small lessons like this are priceless, because you never forget them.

The next part of the work on the flat pegs is done on a 3in (75mm) Velcro sanding disc, clamped in the three-jaw chuck. Start by flattening one side with coarse grit, followed by fine.

To get the side perfectly flat, I get out my sheet of plate glass, taken from an old electric cooker, and place a sheet of 180 abrasive paper on it. Pencil some lines on the peg and

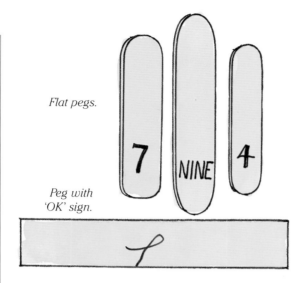

Flat pegs.

Peg with 'OK' sign.

rub over the surface until you can see it's flat. I usually use two more sheets, 240 and 400, then pencil in the OK sign, as shown above.

Back to the Velcro disc (from craft suppliers), where I sand the other side to its correct and even thickness by eye and vernier calliper, but chiefly the former.

For larger or special name plates, where precise uniformity is required, I have another method which would hardly be tolerated in regulations.

I fix up my big cutter, which I call a hub, and set my little saw table below it, adjusting the height to whatever thickness I used by trial and error. I fix a small fence on the side, almost touching the cutter, and the plate to be planed is pushed through from the back with a pusher operated safely from the side.

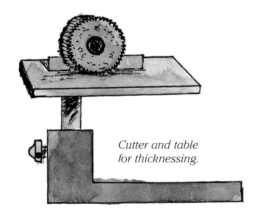

Cutter and table for thicknessing.

The dangerous area is the front of the cutter, of course, but you needn't approach that part. Again, it's a job where you need foot control, because it's done by feel, and the work would seize up in no time with fixed speed. The cutter leaves a rough surface which is soon smoothed to whatever grade of finish is needed, upon the glass.

The length and width of the pegs is achieved with precision on the sanding disc, using a vernier calliper, but the perfectly flat edges are done on the glass, obliterating the pencil mark as before.

The rounded ends are shaped delicately on the sanding disc, holding each one horizontally and moving it lightly round the curve.

A fine disc then replaces the coarse one, and the ends are nicely and accurately finished by holding the peg upright and sliding the curve down and around from each side. By taking care, it isn't necessary to use the glass for the ends.

I have another useful aid for the edges of flat work which would be impaired if polished on the buff. This is a solid felt mop, 8 x 1in (200 x 25mm) thick, mounted on a boxwood arbor. I use Cannings Crown or Lustre on it, little and often, as with a normal buff.

FELT MOP

With the felt mop, the edges can be perfectly polished, after a little practice, for it's easy to burn the edge if you use undue pressure.

Here again, high speed is a killer – you *must* have foot control. The rounded ends are applied to the felt end-wise, as they were on the sanding disc.

The flats polish with jewel-like lustre on the 8 x 1in (200 x 25mm) diameter calico mop, made by Cannings of Birmingham. If you buy a mop and can't get any sense out of it, this is because they have to be 'worked in'.

Tighten the buff fully on its conical screw and start it at top speed. Then, with an old sharp scraper of little value to you – one that is useless for good turning – set up a tee rest and turn the buff, left to right and right to left.

In no time, long threads from the cloth will bristle all around the periphery. Stop, and with a lighted candle, burn off the threads as you slowly turn the buff round by hand, ensuring that you don't burn the cloth.

IF YOU buy a mop and can't get any sense out of it, this is because they have to be 'worked in'

After several turning and burning sessions, the buff should be ready for use. Using some compo, polish a rough piece of wood with it until the buff is clean and ready for use.

Buffs which are stitched – and, of course, cheaper – lack 'give' and are therefore too hard and intractable for my liking. The unstitched 8in (200mm) x 60 fold are what I use and recommend.

A GOOD POLISH

For any work that needs a good polish, rather than an applied lacquer or finish you daren't give to children, the harmless and blameless buff is your best friend.

Many turners prefer their tool handles unpolished, but I like mine buff polished, because they are cleaner and feel better. I blush as I write this, because I still have some disgraceful ancient handles. But they happen to be favourites. They are well-polished disgraceful handles though.

My usual finish for hardwoods is three grades of abrasive paper, Black Bison wax on 0000 steel wool, followed by the calico buff with Crown or Lustre compo, and a final gloss with a 6in (150mm) Swansdown buff, dressed with White Porthos. For the latter – if you wished to be that fussy – you'd have to go to Walshes of Clerkenwell or Cannings.

FINDING CUTTERS

A reader rang me recently, to ask where he could buy rotary burrs, files and cutters, as he had chess knights to carve. He said he had been considering using routing cutters.

This is *not* a good idea, as the wicked teeth, so excellent in the router, are things to keep fingers well away from. I advised him to try Simbles, The Broadway, Watford. Their fine tool catalogue is loaded with an assortment of hard-to-find items, including carving burrs both expensive and cheap. The cheap ones are fine for wood, plastics, bone etc.

The shapes shown here are all useful, but there may be others needed that you'll have to make by hand. It's usual, when contemplating toolmaking, to think of hardened steel as essential. But far from it!

We are working soft materials, therefore the softer steels – or indeed any old iron or brass – will not only cut very adequately, but will be

Carving burrs.

easy to hand-turn to the shape wanted, and can be filed up afterwards.

TINY CUTTERS

Some tiny little cutters, that could be turned and filed from soft bolts or nails in a few minutes, will cost a fiver and work no better. One of my best vee cutters, of about ¾in (20mm) diameter, was knocked up by Bertram 40 years ago, from brass.

It was quickly and crudely done with a triangular needle file, so that anyone doubting their ability would at once exclaim, 'Oh! I could do *that!*' So long as it cuts, the surface finish is unimportant, because you go over the carved work with scrapers and abrasives afterwards.

Cutters you buy are like turning tools, with lots of different shapes you don't want, while the shapes you *do* you must make yourself. 'Twas ever thus, but it's half the fun.

If you turn a vee cutter like the brass one, ¾in (20mm), simply file teeth on each side, sloping forward, close together, and as even as you can get them so they come to points – they'll cut all right.

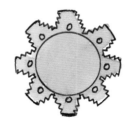

Vandyke cutter.

Another cutter for decoration is a similar large vee but, having turned it, make a series of vee cuts on either side with a chaser (screw tool) or a flat point tool. Then file teeth each side. You don't need skill to do it, I say emphatically, and you'll be delighted with the decorative Vandykes you can produce.

Many a person has joined the Society of Ornamental Turners and laid out thousands of pounds on an ornamental lathe and tools, changing hands for the proverbial king's

ransom today – just to make a Vandyke pattern that *you* can make out of mild steel or brass in 30 minutes.

I've been asked to make these cutters, and although I had every intention of obliging, I don't think I'll ever find the time. Why? Because if I make them, you won't get half the satisfaction that will be yours if you do. And believe me, mine won't be any better than yours.

SPEAR DRILLS

A loyal fan has asked me to give a mench to spear drills. I thought of them when I read a fine article by a turner who, while hollowing deeply, found himself having to deal with what he called a dreaded cone.

My answer is spear drills used with the armrest. The left shoulder, which exerts the force upon the rest (in which the spear drill is cradled) is one too many for ye dreaded cone, you'll find.

I've watched admiringly as good woodturners hollow out vessels with ease, skill and gusto, but I don't try to imitate them because the pressure would jerk my work out of the cup chucks I normally use.

I'm so used to grabbing my spear drills and taking the easy way, I doubt I shall change now. I don't know if they are still made. I have some, up to ¼in (6mm), which are home-made, and larger ones, up to ⅝in (15mm), made by Holtzapffel and Deyerlein, around 1820. They are worth forging from silver steel, if you have the means of heating the steel to a cherry red and hammering the end flat. Grind it as shown above right, with care and accuracy. An alternative shape is also shown in the drawings, and might be useful for some jobs.

Heat the drill to red again and quench for 2in (50mm) or so in thin oil. Take it out and quickly wipe clean. Rub a piece of abrasive paper or emery cloth over the tool end so that you can observe heat colours travelling up to the point.

Spear drills.

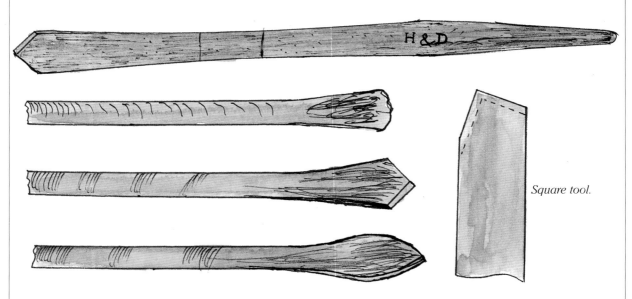

Square tool.

When the point reaches a pale straw colour (and before it goes dark) plunge it back in the oil. Then you can finish sharpening the drill on the oilstone. I think you'll be delighted with it.

It's best when you have a range of varying sizes, which makes the work of the drill, and the driller, very easy. For hollow ware, the initial boring with large spear drills speeds the work and obviates cones.

It's essential to begin with an accurate countersink made with the square tool, shown above. Start drilling with a small drill upon the

IT'S BY no means certain that the goods you buy will be better than those you make

armrest, as this 'persuades' it to go in dead true.

Continue through your range, using the armrest for each drill and for the ensuing hollowing tools. Some of my old drills are quite soft and incapable of being hardened. Perhaps they came out of the Ark! At all events, they come in handy, as even soft metal will cut wood.

I got an engineer to make my saw table when I first started, but often such tables (as for pushing the tablets under the cutter) can be fashioned from hardwood, especially if it's for intermittent work.

DON'T WASTE MONEY

The rule is – don't waste money (unless you are loaded) if you can manage from the materials you have on hand. It's by no means certain that the goods you buy will be better than those you make. In my experience – quite the reverse!

Chapter 20 ● *Help and* INSPIRATION

Above 'The clack o' the belts below.'

One bleak, winter's morning in early December, as I tramped through the frozen meadows with my old dog, I tried to work the magic spell that opens the door to my next *Notes from the Turning Shop*.

Mallards and seagulls were dabbling noisily among the reeds, where the water hadn't frozen. The bare branches of black poplars and blackthorn contrasted with the green gold of willows and scarlet rosehips. Dark green,

withered nettles and light-coloured grasses peeped above the snow. Looking at the scene with a water colourist's eye, it wasn't nearly as bleak as I'd first thought.

What a contrast to the day before, when I'd cut and soaked some old, thin, coarse-grained ivory pegs from can waste, only to find, upon turning them, that they were discoloured and the grain was picking up excessively.

I decided they wouldn't do and, as it approached lunchtime, glanced at the shop's

127

thermometer – it was 43 blooming degrees Fahrenheit, (6°C), and I wisely decided I'd had enough for the day.

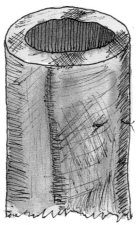

Ivory can waste.

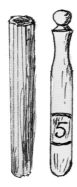

Ivory 'can' cut for pegs.

I usually find in turning, as in many other aspects of life, that when things go wrong, it's best to try something else and return to the problem later. In this case, when the pegs had dried out, they turned quite passably and I need not have worried.

LETTERS

After lunch, I got out my box of Bertram's letters, containing 22 years of my father's 'notes from the turning shop' – and the river bank, viz, 'Talking of fishing, I have been out this morning in the glorious sunshine (13 December '48) and although I did not get anything except an eel and daddy Ruff I had a good time. I did hook a good fish, but the rod was in the rest and I did not strike. I just picked the rod up and the blighter wriggled himself off, but if I hadn't been too lazy I could have got some fish.'

ECONOMY is a necessity if a turner is to make a living

I noted the large quantity of work we'd accomplished during '48 and '49, he at Badsey in the Cotswolds and me in London. That's how I came to have that wonderful box of letters, some of which I'll quote at random later.

First, though, I'd like to tell you how I enlisted Bertram's help in supplying me with a couple of gross of trumpet ends for long, two-piece cigarette tubes I was turning.

These pieces were cut from the small stuff I'd accumulated, remembering that economy is a necessity if a turner is to make a living. The ends were hubbed to fit a boxwood plug in an iron cup chuck. The well-chalked end was tapped in firmly with a 1½lb. (680g) ball pein hammer, and the trumpet shape turned with a ¼in (6mm) gouge, round tool and square tool. I bored the hole with a ⅛in (3mm) spear drill and opened with an accurately-sized one, on the armrest, of course.

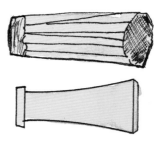

Ivory trumpet end and blank.

Bertram wrote to me on 4 October, '48: 'Have sent this morning one gross of mounts. The other gross will follow in a few days. I now have nine chess sets to make, but have to do another 13 dozen tubes for Comoy this week, or else! I made a gross last week.

'Bob is helping me while he is waiting for his post and he did the major portion of your tops. I think you'll find them OK . . . '

Bob is my learned brother – a BSc, who spent his working life as a scientist but, like all the male Joneses, seems to have been a turner at some time in his life. My older sister Dorothy also proved adept, turning five dozen cord pulls an hour.

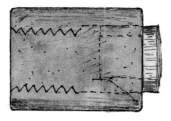

Iron cup chuck with boxwood plug.

Flat drill.

Bertram's next letter arrived a week later. He wrote: 'The trumpets always were a rotten job to reverse, the only way is to open the chuck almost straight and then you have to do a lot of cussing. But, it's all in the game.

'I enclose invoice H/W which you will see is three halfpence more. These took a lot of ivory, being ⁹⁄₁₆in (14mm) as against ½in (12.7mm) for ordinary tubes. I hope that will be OK – if not, cross it off . . . '

I used the rounded end of the ball pein hammer to gently drive the top into the boxwood chuck. The cussing refers to when they fly out – usually at crucial moments. This is the hardwood and ivory turner's greatest challenge, however long one has been at it, though I must say that, due to long experience, the job was 100% safe.

At my last demo, at Sandon, a boxwood rattle came out of the cup chuck several times during the turning, due to carelessness, but survived. To re-fix it in the chuck I used my 'magic' boxwood hammer, but the trumpets needed more force, so I placed a piece of hardwood over the end as a protection, and whanged it in with the heavy hammer. The 'butterfly's wing' touch of the tools I often mention is largely, but by no means always, due to the necessity of avoiding sending work flying out of the chuck.

But, to continue my dip into Bertram's letters: 28 February, '49: '. . . a bloke in Exchange and Mart has 18 reams of glasscloth to sell at £4 a ream (480 sheets). It's not quite as good as Oakeys, working out at 2d a sheet (¹⁄₁₂₀ of a quid).

'I think I'll buy a ream and then you can help me use it up as you want it. Don't grumble about old Hammers' bones until you see the rotten stuff I have to cut up.

'They use some scientific method of extracting the fat or, as they call it, "Organics". The consequence is there's no nature left in the bone – it would make our grandfathers weep!'

I hardly ever have to use bone today. I think the butcher is the best bet.

12 February, '49: '. . . I had an order for a lot of the usual tripe from Barratt; spoons, dice, toothpicks, nail trimmers, letter openers, etc. Also, various repairs.'

1 January, '49: '. . . don't worry if you are temporarily out of orders. I often am. Just go on getting ready for the rush. While I think of it, can you get me an old file for a square tool? I'm down to nix.'

Commenting on my encounter with a Centrix lathe, which didn't even boast a collar behind the mandrel nose, so that one blow with the hammer sent the mandrel back through the bearing and pulley, he wrote on 2 January, '49:

'I don't think much of these cheap lathes, which won't stand up to continuous work. You want something of substance. Anyway, what I've got will last me my time out, and perhaps you as well. There's one thing in their favour – they will stand a clout!'

Two-piece ivory trumpet tube.

SHORT NOTE

5 December, '48: 'Just a short note to give you the weekly report. I've done three sets of chess, dyed today and will pack tomorrow. I have also had another order from Lindop for ventilator fittings which they say they are desperately in need of, so it don't seem as if I shall get any time to myself before Xmas.

'I expect you are in the same boat. The trouble with our work is it's all bits of this, that and the other. There's nothing straightforward about it; you can't get any help.

'My next job is six dozen ebony stethoscope ends for Carsberg, which I promised to do for 6 December. Then I have dice, rattles, tooth-picks, studs, paper knives, and letter slitters for B, not to mention necklaces for callers.

'It's been a lovely week. I ought to have been out fishing, but must wait until after Xmas, I suppose. Hope you are going on all right.'

A week before, Bertram had written: 'Glad to hear you have plenty of work. I shall not be able to do all my orders before Xmas, but I'll keep pegging away. Carsberg sent an order for ebony chesspieces and I also had an order for a gross of stethoscope eartips from Billings, of Manchester.

'As you say, when we are slack they never

Bertram's chess sets were all hand carved on a plain lathe.

want anything. I suppose it's the natural cussedness of things . . .

'P.S. I had my Income Tax demand. I've got to pay 15 shillings in two instalments. I suppose they're going to build a couple of dreadnoughts!'

TEN YEARS ON

Let's go forward 10 years, to 13 October, '58: '. . . the trouble with work for people like Chalmers is that they want stuff that takes a lot of ivory of the best quality, and by the time you've bought it you're lucky if you get your money back – and your profit is a bit of waste ivory for which you have no use.

'Regarding the Society of Ornamental Turners show, you can't expect any work from that. They are only playing at it!

'I smiled at Howes' 25 hours to make a Chinese ball. When I have to make one for an old Cantonese set I get 10 shillings (one hour). The proof of a craftsman is, "one who can earn a living at it".

'We have had the rains back again today, but Sunday was glorious. You can't beat fishing to make you forget your own and the world's troubles. Hope you go on all right. We are OK at this end.'

17 September, '58: 'Regarding small chessmen, as I mentioned, this type is now defunct. In the old days, grosses were made,

all out of waste ivory or bone. They are knocking about in all sorts of homes and, as they were not valued, the kids had them to play with, so a complete set is a rarity now.

'They retailed at about 15 shillings (at least £75 today). I should want £8 for mine in that size. I've never had an order for them, but have faked up and completed plenty of similar sets (antique of course).

'I don't think you would sell them only as repros of antique sets. I can't imagine fellows turning the pawns for 12 shillings a gross (an old penny, 1/240th of £1, each), but it was looked on as a good job in them days.

'How about bone cribbage pegs at 1/3d a gross (one shilling and threepence, 1/16 of £1 per gross). Then they wonder why there is a shortage of skilled turners! Of course, that was against foreign competition, but that don't apply now, the poor bastards are all starved to death and the modern generation has got more sense.

'I am sending you a parcel of bits and pieces. The stud earrings are all 4/– (four shillings) and the carved variety with silver mounts, 12/6. Round brooches are 5/–, oval 7/6, the flower one 10/– and the drops 7/6.

'I get 15/– for rattles. The small screwed box is 30/–, and the condiment set, £4.

'I also include two very old patterns of parasol handles. The men who carved these got 8d (¹⁄₃₀ of £1) an hour. You will notice one in bone, turned on a foot lathe. Also two bone knobs, for which I got 5/6 a gross, and liked it! I suppose insanity runs in the family.'

2 June, '55: 'I'm glad you are going in for chessmen, as there seems to be a steady demand for them. I still get only £12 for the Staunton club size – a 4½in (115mm) king, in best African ivory, of which you have the patterns.

'I know the price of ivory is still rising, but I don't like to put the screw on with Hammond, as he's been a decent customer. I don't think you need have anything to worry about, for the turned parts are quite ordinary – the only trouble is the knights.

'Of course, in a factory a turner would just do the turning and there would be a sawyer to cut the stuff and a carver to do the carving. A polisher would finish the job.

'Then, presumably, there would be a qualified chemist with a string of degrees who would undertake the staining of the reds. But in our trade we have to do the jolly lot!

'I'll write to you again later, with any little hints I can think of (although I don't expect they will be new to you), when I can sit down comfortable and think things out, perhaps this weekend. It's jolly cold sitting in my shop and I must get on. So long and all the best, Dad.'

Lummy! He was just like me, wasn't he?

UNDERVALUED

It's terrible to think that the assembly line, mass-produced job of Jaques cost more than Bertram's hand-made pieces,

which are fetching thousands at auctions now! Fortunately, he was so quick he made a fair profit.

Here's one, 3 April, '61: 'B . . . is only too glad to get repairs of old sets, for which he has clients who will pay almost any price. These old sets are looked upon as the work of the Old Masters, which cannot be reproduced.

'Little do they realize that the poor bastards got about 6d an hour, worked 10 hours a day and liked it; it was good fun treadling a lathe under a corrugated iron roof in temperatures up to 90°F (32°C) with the guv'nor telling you what a B fool you were!

'But you can learn a lot from these repairs and they are not beyond the capacity of chaps like you to reproduce. What they could do we can do better. It's just a matter of price. What was once a trade is now an art . . . '

ORNATE SETS

Provided Bertram got what he felt he had honestly earned, the destination of his work never bothered him. That was his client's business. In his later years, up to 1969 when he died, aged 84, he made many ornate sets, some of which took a month. Usually he got them photographed, but a number were rushed out before there was time to take them into the Evesham photographer.

But I've seen them in books and can vouch that there are collectors who prize 'centuries old' English, French, Italian, or Turkish sets that were made by old Bertram, and none the worse for that. I'd be proud to own any one of them – if I could afford it!

King from Bertram's Dieppe set.

Right *Offcuts too numerous to mention.*

Health *and* SAFETY

I have a very popular workshop because it is so impossibly cluttered that it makes everyone with less clutter feel virtuous. Tony Boase told me that when he showed a slide of it at a seminar in Ireland a cheer went up! It's taken over 30 years to achieve this splendid effect.

There are open belts, an open grinder, an open circular saw and open carving cutters. But clumsy and forgetful though I often am, I feel safer here than when I venture outside. The open belts are either well out of the way or foot-controlled. The grinder is foot-controlled and rather slow. The circular saw is foot-

134

Above A place for everything – and everything all over the place!